StressCosts
Stress-Cures

Hi, Robert. Thanks for all your support, and for your friendship.

Ravi

Ravi Tangri

Printed in Victoria, Canada

National Library of Canada Cataloguing in Publication Data

Tangri, Ravi, 1961-
        Stress costs, stress cures / Ravi Tangri.
Includes bibliographical references and index.
ISBN 1-4120-0074-2
        1. Job stress. I. Title.
HF5548.85.T35 2003   158.7'2   C2003-901520-3

TRAFFORD

This book was published *on-demand* in cooperation with Trafford Publishing.
On-demand publishing is a unique process and service of making a book available for retail sale to the public taking advantage of on-demand manufacturing and Internet marketing. **On-demand publishing** includes promotions, retail sales, manufacturing, order fulfilment, accounting and collecting royalties on behalf of the author.

Suite 6E, 2333 Government St., Victoria, B.C. V8T 4P4, CANADA

Phone	250-383-6864	Toll-free	1-888-232-4444 (Canada & US)
Fax	250-383-6804	E-mail	sales@trafford.com
Web site	www.trafford.com	TRAFFORD PUBLISHING IS A DIVISION OF TRAFFORD HOLDINGS LTD.	
Trafford Catalogue #03-0437		www.trafford.com/robots/03-0437.html	

10   9   8   7   6   5   4   3   2

Note to Readers

You have permission to post, email, print and pass along the electronic (PDF) version of this document for free to anyone you like, as long as you make no changes or edits to its contents or digital format. The right to bind this and sell it as a book, however, is strictly reserved. If you don't want to e-mail this file, you can e-mail a link to www.Stress-Cures.com, which will allow the recipient to download it.

You can find this entire document, along with a spreadsheet for calculating the costs of stress according to the enclosed formula, and other support information at www.Stress-Cures.com. You can also, if you wish, purchase the paperback version of this book from that location.

This version of **StressCosts Stress-Cures** is current as of March 31, 2003. After that date, please go to www.Stress-Cures.com to get updated versions.

How to Use This Book

The most critical chapters of **StressCosts Stress-Cures** are:

- Chapter 1 (*The Bottom Line*), which summarizes the essence of the book
- Chapter 2 (*The StressCosts Formula*™), which provides the formula you can use to calculate what stress costs your organization's bottom line
- Chapter 6 (*How to Regain Productivity*), which outlines the two approaches to recover productivity lost to stress in your organization

From that point on, you can read the chapters that are most relevant to you.

This book's breakthrough is Chapter 2 (*The StressCosts Formula*™), where you will find the formula into which you can plug your own organization's information to calculate your own corporate costs of stress.

You can download a copy of the research report *What Stress Costs* that was used to derive the StressCosts Formula™ at www.Stress-Cures.com. At this web site you will also find other resources including an Excel spreadsheet that will allow you to apply the formula to your own organization.

The formula uses percentages so it is applicable to any currency. Financial figures provided in this book generally refer to the currency of the country in question. In the case of dollars, Canadian data is expressed in Canadian dollars and American findings are expressed in American dollars.

Chapter 3 (*Your Hard Costs of Stress*) provides more background and detail on the StressCosts Formula™. Chapter 4 (*Understanding Stress*) explains what stress is and how it impacts both individuals and organizations. Chapter 5 (*What Causes Stress*) identifies the root cause of organizational stress.

Chapter 6 (*How to Regain Productivity*) outlines the strategies for recovering productivity lost to stress and shows their bottom-line impact. Chapter 7 (*How to Build Systems That Work*) shows you how to address the systemic roots of stress. Finally, Chapter 8 (*Leading the Way*) provides five case studies of leaders who show how theory is put into practice in real life.

Acknowledgements

First and foremost, I would like to thank and acknowledge my wife and partner, Kathy, for all her support, both in editing and in making sure Chrysalis ran effectively while I focused on pulling this book together. My thanks also to Gail Godreau for helping me sift through the piles of research to find the most valid and usable elements, and to my long-time friend Stuart Smith for editing my work.

Thanks to Michael Basch, my friend, mentor and colleague, for writing the Foreword to this book, and for the systems framework, Value-Added Curve, and C.E.O. Goals concepts detailed in Chapter 7.

I would also like to recognize all those who conducted the research that has been accumulated in this book, most notably the recent breakthroughs provided in the 2001 National Work-Life Conflict Study by Chris Higgins and Linda Duxbury.

And, of course, my thanks to all of the people in our *Genesis* and *Thriving In Chaos* programs, who taught me so much and showed me why this book is so important and necessary.

Table of Contents

Stress-Cures

Foreword

Few would argue that management action is necessary to tackle negative workplace stress, however it is like motherhood and apple pie. "Of course I want to reduce negative stress, but I, as a corporate leader, will not take it seriously until I have a strong understanding that stress is hurting sales and profits." To a great extent, it is a known problem with unknown quantification and solution.

Until **StressCosts Stress-Cures** by Ravi Tangri.

One problem when considering this issue is that stress can yield higher performance in certain situations. An athlete is under stress every time she or he enters a competition. A driven employee about to close a big sale is under stress and the adrenaline is flowing caused by the passion of opportunity.

The problem arises when you keep applying this pressure day after day, month after month, and year after year. Then the chemicals that drove us to higher performance start to poison our body and we start an addictive downward spiral that can be incredibly difficult to recover from. We push harder and harder, and our productivity gets worse and worse.

Like positive and negative cholesterol, stress has two sides.

Identifying and reducing negative workplace stress is what this book is all about. It is clear that we, as a business community have gone beyond the positive effect of stress and moved into the dark territory of negative stress that affects the passion and productivity of our employees, and the bottom line of corporate performance.

This is the opposite of the Olympian or sales person rising to excellence that goes beyond even what they thought was possible. Events like these happen occasionally, not several times every day.

It is the debilitating stress of feeling powerless and insignificant to those around you and, as important, feeling that you don't count or don't make any difference in your world.

Ravi Tangri tackles the issues of stress in the workplace from both an analytical and personal power perspective. He has recognized and proven that reducing negative workplace stress has a very positive influence on sick time and productivity. He has also recognized and proven that an employee's sense of loss of personal power leads to negative stress and loss of performance.

Ravi Tangri gives leaders the understanding of the specific costs and causes of negative workplace stress and then goes on to show in simple, practical terms how to take negative stress out of the workplace.

Fred Smith, CEO and founder of FedEx, put it another way: "Give a person a sense of control over their own destiny (personal power) and they'll give you everything they've got – and more."

Quantifying the costs of stress and the focus that comes from that quantification reminds me of my last project at FedEx – building the superhub in Memphis, Tennessee.

We knew intuitively that on time departures were a critical ingredient to success, but the sorting costs per package was the prime productivity measure – the stockholder value so to speak.

The reality was that the hub could dramatically reduce their cost per package, but a late airplane arriving at Newark airport would dramatically increase the delivery cost per package far more than efficiencies gained in the hub.

The point is that, until we put a dollar value on late departures, on-time departures would not get the management attention they deserved – both in terms of hub design and daily management attention.
As a result, prior to the final design of the hub systems, I commissioned a project to determine the cost of a late minute at the hub. After some research, it was determined that for every minute the sort went down late, it cost the delivery system $10,000. That's a lot of money for a lost minute caused by poor design or management.

Foreword

This conclusion led us to build in very sophisticated back-up systems and manage the sort in minute-by-minute increments.

What has all this to do with stress?

Immediately before us is the invisible profit killer called negative stress. We cannot see through the immediate tasks that face everyone in business today to the causal factors. We need to put a handle on costs of stress that relates to the bottom line. Once we have a clear understanding of the real costs of stress, we will then move to reduce and eliminate it in the workplace. It will be a natural reaction.

Ravi Tangri in this book has put numbers to these intuitive and now proven conclusions about stress and its real revenue and profit impact.

I have known Ravi for a decade now as a business associate, close friend and as my personal coach. He embodies the rare combination of a scientist and a social change master.

As a scientist, he is not satisfied with the usual platitudes of opinion from those who want to increase the importance of their work in the eyes of others.

As a social change master, he is not blind to the real costs and social importance of negative stress in the workplace.

Ravi Tangri has defined the bottom line effects of stress. He has defined the $10,000 a minute that we all need to have in front of us constantly to make clear decisions to attack rather than ignore what is arguably the biggest single problem in business today.

This book will help you identify the actual cost of negative stress in your company and then show you how to take the simple, low cost, steps to reduce and ultimately eliminate it.

Michael D. Basch
Founding Partner, Federal Express, and author of *CustomerCulture*

Prelude

"I just don't know what to do. I've put together some incredible strategies, but things change so fast that we can't make any headway – and it's getting faster all the time. I feel like I'm a rat on a treadmill flying through a maze. I can't control where I'm going, and some idiot's playing games with the speed control."

Dave's frustration poured through. It had been a rough morning, with last month's results falling far short of projections. The plan he had developed had been perfect – it should have worked like clockwork, but something was wrong. The results were far short of expectations and if they didn't turn around soon, he'd have to do something radical to reach the targets he'd set out and make plan.

"I'm sorry," he said, looking at his friends. "We haven't seen each other in months, and I'm off ranting about my problems. It's just that things are so volatile. We develop a program focused on customer service, and the competition moves in another direction. We push a new product line, and we can't get it out in time. We reorganize to meet the market's needs, and the market changes. And then I still have to make plan. Sometimes it seems like you just can't win anymore."

"I know exactly what you mean," said Pat. "Work isn't the way it used to be. I can't even remember the last time I went home before 7 or 8, and even then it seems like I'm further behind."

"Tell me about it," chimed in Alex. "But that's the way the world is today, and that's why we get the big bucks – and the big chair. You've got to work harder and faster just to survive."

"Easy for you to say, Alex," said Pat. "You're running your own business, and Dave's the president of his show. What you say goes. We're like the poor stepchild in HR.

"I thought it would be different when I went from the private sector to the public sector, but it's all the same. We're supposed to pick up the pieces from all the changes that you guys make, but we've got nothing to work with. And guess who has to clean up the mess from all the layoffs and cutbacks that get handed down?"

"Whoa – relax, Pat," countered Dave. "Sometimes there just isn't any choice. Salary and benefits are the biggest chunk of expenses. If we're going to keep our heads above water, that's got to take a hit. And I don't always get the budget I want. That's why I have to be on top of the game to keep up. I just wish some of the people in our organization would realize that they have to as well. Productivity's just going down the tubes – and that's with the people who're staying."

"Sometimes it seems we don't need to have layoffs," added Alex. "Sometimes they're bailing out faster than we want. They just can't handle it. Of course, then there's the people you *wish* would leave, who never do."

"Oh yeah," said Pat. "Sometimes I feel like I've got a split personality – getting packages ready for some people while I'm out recruiting for others. It just never stops. What about you, Sharon? How are you holding up with all this?"

Sharon had been sitting back listening to the conversation. She slowly sat up in her chair as she became the focus of attention for her three old friends who had been totally fixated on each other until now.

"I'm not really sure what to say, actually." She paused. "Things are actually going really well. We've got slow, steady growth, and the team's great. I'm having a great time."

"Oh, come on, Shar," said Dave, "sure things are great and you have a great team. We all do. But you can't tell me you're not feeling the pressure of all these changes!"

"We're changing, yes, but not in the way you're talking about. We're pretty solid on our plans. We do our homework, set our strategy, and work the plan, and it delivers. I mean, sure, there are tweaks along the way, but that's what our job is – to keep things on track. After all, we're responsible for the results we generate, aren't we?"

Prelude

"Well yes, but I can't be responsible for our competition or for the changes in our market, or even for one of our departments that can't deliver what it promised. What do you do when sales come up short, or production screws up?" Dave was really focused on Sharon now.

"Then we learn, and we move forward. We all keep in touch with what the others are doing, so there are rarely surprises. And we're all involved in the development of the strategy, so we've rarely committed to what we can't deliver."

"Give me a break, Shar," said Alex. "Sure, everyone 'commits' to the plan, but somebody always comes up short. You're talking fairy tales here. Next thing you're going to tell me you're home for dinner every night."

"I am, actually. And so are most people in the organization."

"Right – and how do you keep up with the work?"

"Actually, we probably have more productivity than you. No – listen up," she put in as Dave snorted. "You started this, now you listen. What's your absenteeism rate like? Did you know that some companies have found that almost two-thirds of absenteeism is the result of stress? At least 19% is directly due to stress. That doesn't even include all the illnesses coming out of stress – heart disease, depression, you name it. And then there's all the problems and conflicts people have with their personal lives because of their workload."

"Hold on," cut in Dave, "that's their personal lives. That's their responsibility, not ours. This is about work."

"It *is* about work, Dave," countered Sharon. "When they have to take time off because of those problems it affects work, plus there's all the lost productivity from stress that nobody's been able to pin down.

"You've already said you have a revolving door for staff for turnover – whether they leave or you lay them off. Nearly half of turnover is because of the stress and pressures you're putting on them with all the changes. Add in all the other costs of accidents, and workers' compensation claims, and put those numbers together, and you've probably got fewer productive hours per employee than we do."

"That's nonsense!"

"No it's not," said Pat. "She's right about all those costs. The trouble is that they don't show up on the P&L. They're hidden, so you never really know how much it really costs you. All you see are the 'savings' from cutting positions, not the impact of that on productivity."

Alex paused for a moment, then said "No. I still don't buy it. Sure, stress and all that other warm and fuzzy stuff has an impact, but it's not that big."

"Alex," responded Sharon, "first of all, it's not 'warm and fuzzy' stuff any more. You can put hard numbers to all that 'warm and fuzzy' stuff – and the payback of all that increased productivity goes straight to your bottom line. You want results? Let's talk bottom line…"

StressCosts

Chapter 1 – The Bottom Line

In 1992, a United Nations report called job stress "the 20th century disease." Shortly afterwards, the World Health Organization (WHO) said that it had become a "world wide epidemic." In the decade since then, ongoing change, mergers, and organizational anorexia due to downsizings and 'rightsizings' has produced a workforce that is working harder, less able to balance work and home, more insecure about their future, far more stressed and far less productive.

Stress costs American businesses more than $300 Billion annually in lost productivity, absenteeism, accidents, employee turnover, and medical, legal and insurance fees, and workers' compensation awards. This is more than 15 times the cost of all strikes combined. In Canada, the annual cost to business is $16 Billion, which is equivalent to 14% of total net profits. Total costs to employers for accidents and work-related ill health in the United Kingdom is £7.3 Billion.

Despite figures like these, many managers are uncomfortable dealing with stress. Part of this discomfort is because stress has always been nebulous and hard to quantify. Partly it's because the causes of stress can link to personal issues not related to the job itself. Some managers believe that these issues have nothing to do with the job, that the employee should deal with them, and that they are barriers to managing effectively.

Those issues impact workers' performance and productivity, and thus the organization's profitability and success. Effective management *demands* that these issues be addressed. Rather than these issues getting *in the way* of good management, good management is *about* dealing effectively with these concerns so employees can realize their full potential. In fact, effective leadership is the key to reducing employee stress and to recovering productivity lost to stress.

StressCosts Stress-Cures shows you how to measure the impact of stress to *your* organization and/or department and identifies the strategies available to you to recover the productivity that has been lost to stress.

The Hard Costs of Stress

The following costs have been substantiated by research and are included in the StressCosts Formula™ in this book:

- 19% of absenteeism
- 40% of turnover (the cost of turnover is 150-250% of the salary benefit envelope for each position)
- 55% of EAP program costs (consult your provider for a more accurate number – it may be higher)
- 30% of short-term disability and long-term disability costs
- 10% of drug plan costs to cover psychotherapeutic drug costs
- 60% of the total cost of workplace accidents
- the total cost of workers' compensation claims and lawsuits due to stress

Making these calculations will provide you with a *conservative* estimate of what stress costs your organization. There are no solid research findings giving accurate costs for the following factors, and so they have not been included in the formula:

- productivity lost owing to stress while the employee is at work
- violence in the workplace including bullying, sexual harassment, and ethnic/racial harassment
- disability and drug plan costs due to illnesses caused by stress (cardiovascular, etc.)

Stress generally has more of an impact on white-collar workers, on employees lower in the organizational ranks, in the services sector, and on women. Everyday small stressors are generally the most damaging. Each one of these catalyzes 1,400 chemical reactions in your body, some of which continue for hours after the stressor that caused it has passed.

Individuals affected by stress smoke more, eat more, have more alcohol and drug-related problems, are less motivated, have more trouble with co-workers, and have more illness. Stress impairs the immune system, and can result in more infectious diseases, chronic respiratory illnesses, high blood pressure, obesity, cardiovascular diseases, gastrointestinal disorders, depression, and cancer.

Chapter 1 – The Bottom Line

What Causes Stress

Causes of stress include increasing workloads and work hours, and a lack of control. These factors can upset employees' work-life balance and increase feelings of helplessness. Generally, employees are more stressed and suffer more ill-effects of stress when they have high demands placed on them, with little control, and/or when they are asked to put in a great deal of effort with little resulting reward.

At the core of these issues is the one and only one factor that accurately predicts whether an employee will be able to effectively manage stressful situations and stay healthy. That factor is his or her sense of personal power. Personal power is your sense of knowing that you have the resources and abilities to handle the issues and challenges that you will encounter. It is the opposite of helplessness.

The greater your personal power, the greater your ability to deal effectively with stressful situations and the greater the chance you will stay healthy. The lower your personal power (and the higher your sense of helplessness), the greater the chance that you will become ill as a result of the stresses you are facing.

How to Recover Productivity Lost to Stress

There are two strategies to enhance the personal power of your employees, and to recover the productivity lost to stress. The first targets your employees directly and helps them build their personal power so they can cope with the stressors that they face. The second approach targets the root cause of stress in organizations, which lies not in your people, but in the culture of your organization itself.

With both approaches, it is essential that you measure the right things to identify what stress is costing you now, and that you measure the impact of your initiatives to show your payback and ROI. Despite the fact that they are readily available, few companies pull out figures such as absenteeism and turnover. If you want to improve your financial performance, you have to measure these 'soft' numbers and their financial impact, and you have to make them count. While most business decisions are based on the 'hard' numbers, financial statements actually hide the impact of both stress and wellness programs.

The first strategy targets your employees directly and generates results fairly quickly. In order to have a real impact, you must use a program that is proven to enhance the personal power of your employees. Traditional stress-management programs fail because they focus on self-care, which has a marginal impact on your ability to deal with stress, and not with personal power. Finding and implementing a program that enhances your employees' personal power can produce measurable and sustainable results in a very short time frame. In fact, it has been shown that effective wellness programs produce an ROI of $1.64 to $6.85 for each dollar invested.

The second approach is more medium- to long-term, and focuses on the roots of stress in your organizational culture and cultural systems. To a large extent your leadership shapes your culture. Traditionally, management has focused more on results and less on people skills. Unfortunately, this focus creates stress, and thus adversely affects results as well. Simply put, organizations that actively support their people outperform those that don't on virtually every financial measure.

Wellness, job satisfaction (which directly impacts profitability), employee commitment, reward, and employees' sense of control are all within the control of the organization. While it was believed that these were all vague, indefinable concepts, hard numbers can be put on these with a wide range of organizational climate and leadership surveys that are available today. You can measure where your organization is, set specific, measurable targets, identify specific behaviours and cultural systems you need to get there, and measure your progress. Once again, it comes down to investing the effort to measure the right things.

While not every organization is ready to examine and rebuild its systems and culture to reach the next level, every organization can help its employees enhance their personal power and cope more effectively with the stressors that they are facing. It is possible to recover the productivity lost to stress. First measure what it's costing you now, measure the factors that are producing stress in your organization, and then decide what action you want to take.

Chapter 2 – The StressCosts Formula™

This chapter integrates comprehensive research into the costs of stress to present a simple formula for calculating the costs of stress to *your* bottom line. The number that you will get will likely be an underestimate, and it will still be significant. As comprehensive as the research is, it is not complete. This formula *only* includes those calculations that have solid findings behind them and, when a range of figures is available, it generally includes the lower end of the range, to be conservative. Chapter 3 gives more detail on the elements of this formula. For a thorough review of the research from which this formula was derived, refer to the special report *What Stress Costs*, which you can download at www.Stress-Cures.com.

For these calculations, use a one-year period for all numbers. Unless otherwise indicated, these steps apply to *every* person in the organization (front-line, management, etc.). Where you have specific data available, replace the given formulas with your data.

Absenteeism

Cost of Absenteeism Due to Stress = (Total of Lost Salary/Benefit Due to Absenteeism) x 19%

1. For each employee, multiply the total number of days they were absent in the year by that employee's average daily cost of salary plus benefits. Add in any additional costs, such as overtime for someone else to work that position.

2. Add together the numbers from step 1 for the total cost of absenteeism over the year and insert it below:

Step 2	Total cost of absenteeism	

3. Multiply the figure in line 2 by 19% to determine the cost of absenteeism *directly* attributable to stress over the year, and enter this number below:

Step 3	Cost of absenteeism directly due to stress **(Step 2 x 19%)**	

Turnover

Cost of Turnover for Front-line Staff = (Total Salary/Benefit Envelope of Positions Vacated) x 150%

Cost of Turnover for Mid. Mgt. & Jr. Sales = (Total Salary/Benefit Envelope of Positions Vacated) x 200%

Cost of Turnover for Senior Managers & Sr. Sales = (Total Salary/Benefit Envelope of Positions Vacated) x 250%

Total Cost of Turnover = (Sum of Front Line, Supervisory, Management and Sales Turnover Costs)

Cost of Turnover Due to Stress = (Total Cost of Turnover) x 40%

4. Identify every non-management employee who is not a sales professional (ie: all front-line staff who are not salespeople) who has left their job for any reason whatsoever over the year.

Chapter 2 – The StressCosts Formula™

5. Add together the salary/benefit envelopes for all of the people identified in step 4.

Step 5	Total of salary/benefit envelopes of front-line employees who have left their jobs	

6. Multiply the figure in step 5 by 150% to calculate the total cost of turnover for front-line employees.

Step 6	Total cost of front-line turnover **(Step 5 x 150%)**	

7. Identify every supervisory, middle management, and junior sales position where the employee has left his/her job in the previous year.

8. Add together the salary/benefit envelopes for all of the positions identified in step 7.

Step 8	Total of salary/benefit envelopes of supervisory, mid. mgt., and jr. sales people who have left their jobs	

9. Multiply the figure in step 8 by 200% to calculate the total cost of turnover for supervisors, middle managers, and junior sales people.

Step 9	Total cost of mid. mgt./jr. sales turnover **(Step 8 x 200%)**	

10. Identify every senior management position and every senior sales position that has been vacated in the past year.

11. Add together the salary/benefit envelopes for all of the positions identified in step 10.

Step 11	Total of salary/benefit envelopes of senior mgt. and sales people who left their jobs	

12. Multiply the figure in step 11 by 250% to calculate the total cost of turnover for senior managers and senior sales professionals for the last year.

Step 12	Total cost of senior mgt./sr. sales turnover **(Step 11 x 250%)**	

13. Add together the figures from steps 6, 9, and 12 to calculate the total costs of turnover for your organization for the last year.

Step 13	Total cost of turnover **(Step 6 + Step 9 + Step 12)**	

14. Multiply the figure from step 13 by 40% to identify the costs of turnover due to stress.

Step 14	Cost of turnover due to stress. **(Step 13 x 40%)**	

14

Chapter 2 – The StressCosts Formula™

EAP Programs

> Cost of EAP Due to Stress = (Total EAP Costs) x 55%

15. Multiply the total cost of EAP programs by 55%.

Step 15	Cost of EAP due to stress **(Total cost of EAP x 55%)**	

Benefits

> Disability Cost Due to Stress = (Total Disability Costs) x 30%
>
> Cost of Psychotherapeutic Drugs = (Total Drug Costs) x 10%

16. Add together the total short-term and long-term disability costs.
    Multiply this total by 30%.

Step 16	Disability cost due to stress **((Total STD and LTD costs)x 30%)**	

17. Multiply the total drug plan costs by 10%.

Step 17	Cost of psychotherapeutic drugs **(Total drug costs x 10%)**	

Workplace Accidents

Cost of Workplace Accidents Due to Stress = (Total Cost of Accidents)
x 60%

18. Calculate the total cost of workplace accidents to the organization.
Multiply this total by 60%.

Step 18	Cost of workplace accidents caused by stress **(Total cost of workplace accidents x 60%)**	

Workers' Compensation Claims and Law Suits

19. Calculate the total cost of workers' compensation claims and
lawsuits related to stress, and mental health issues.

Step 19	Total cost of workers' compensation claims and lawsuits related to stress/mental health	

Total Cost of Stress

20. Add together the figures for steps 3, 14, 15, 16, 17, 18, and 19 to
calculate the total cost of stress to your organization over the year.

Step 20	Insert total cost of absenteeism due to stress (Step 3)	
	Insert total cost of turnover due to stress (Step 14)	
	Insert cost of EAP programs due to stress (Step 15)	
	Insert disability cost due to stress (Step 16)	
	Insert cost of psychotherapeutic drugs (Step 17)	
	Insert cost of accidents caused by stress (Step 18)	
	Insert workers comp. & law suit costs (Step 19)	
	Total cost of stress to your organization (Step 3 + Step 14 + Step 15 + Step 16 + Step 17 + Step 18 + Step 19)	

This formula includes the costs of:
- absenteeism *directly* due to stress
- turnover
- EAP programs
- short-term and long-term disability costs due to stress
- drug costs for psychotherapeutics
- workplace accidents
- workers' compensation claims
- cost of law suits related to stress and mental health issues

It does not include the following costs:
- lost productivity while employees are at work
- violence in the workplace
- absence due to illness caused by stress (ie: cardiovascular disease, etc.)
- absence due to work-life conflict

- drug costs for illnesses produced by stress (cardiovascular, etc.)

The bulk of the research used to develop this formula was conducted in the United States, Canada and Europe. These data support the formula in North America and Europe and the use of percentages allows easy applicability to any currency.

Chapter 3 – Your Hard Costs of Stress

The StressCosts Formula™ provides you with a quick way to calculate the impact of stress on your bottom line. This chapter will flesh out the picture for each of the elements of the formula, as well as on those areas that are not included in the formula.

Absenteeism

At least one in five of all last-minute no-shows come from stress, which means that more than 1 million workers are absent from work in the United States every day due to stress. The United Kingdom's HSE states that stress-related illnesses alone are responsible for a loss of 6.5 million working days each year, costing employers £370 Million and society overall as much as £3.75 Billion.

Male, low-tenure, part-time, and high-wage employees are less likely to be absent. Employees on shift-work, those with greater sick leave entitlements, and those with better labor market options are more likely to be absent. Employees who reported stress due to interpersonal relationships, job control, and management practices are also more likely than others to be absent for six or more days. Although costs differ somewhat between organizations, the cost of absenteeism can easily amount to 1.5 to 2 times the employee's wage for each day that he misses.

There is a wide range of estimates for the percentage of absenteeism that is due to stress. A 1997 study by one large corporation discovered that 60% of employee absences could be traced to psychological problems resulting from stress. The European Agency for Safety and Health at Work reported that more than half of the 550,000,000 workdays lost annually because of absenteeism in the United States were caused by stress. The Confederation of British Industry (CBI) has stated that approximately one-third of sickness absenteeism was owing to stress.

CCH Incorporated's 2001 Unscheduled Absence Survey reflects the experiences of a cross-section of American organizations representing 1, 371, 261 employees. It found that the average absenteeism rate increased from 2.1% in 2000 to 2.2% in 2001, and the average per-employee cost of absenteeism rose significantly from $610 in 2000 to $755 in 2001. Overall, the direct costs associated with unscheduled absences increased by 24%.

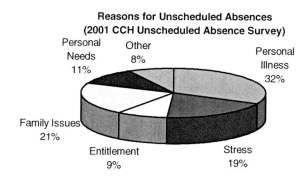

Reasons for Unscheduled Absences
(2001 CCH Unscheduled Absence Survey)

Personal Needs 11%
Other 8%
Personal Illness 32%
Family Issues 21%
Entitlement 9%
Stress 19%

Only 32% of unscheduled absences were used for personal illness. Family issues caused 21%, stress caused 19%, personal needs caused 11%, 9% were caused by an entitlement mentality, and 8% resulted from other causes. These results were in stark contrast to the 1995 version of this survey, which showed that 45% of unscheduled absences were caused by personal illness, and only 6% were directly due to stress.

While there are estimates of stress-related absenteeism ranging as high as 60% of absenteeism, the more conservative figure of 19% from the CCH research is used in the StressCosts Formula™. These numbers don't take into account absenteeism owing to illness caused by stress, so it is likely an underestimate.

Turnover

Forty percent of turnover is due to stress. One in five employees have quit a job in the past because of stress, and one in ten workers are looking for a new position at any given time. Despite the fact that more companies are using both monetary tactics and non-monetary tactics (casual dress, flexible work hours, etc.) to retain employees, half of companies experienced increased turnover in 2000, and one in three reported that their retention methods were failing.

Chapter 3 – Your Hard Costs of Stress

Many estimates of the actual costs of turnover have ranged from 10% to 25% of the employee's salary. These estimates, however, are far short of the real costs of turnover because they generally only look at the direct costs, such as the time for recruitment, selection, and formal training for the new hire. These visible costs have been found to comprise only 10-15% of the total costs of turnover. The total costs of turnover can be broken down into termination costs, vacancy costs, hiring costs, training costs, and economic costs.

Termination costs include:
* cost of terminating the employee and separation pay
* cost of exit interviewer's time
* administrative, accounting and legal costs

Vacancy costs include:
* overtime
* temporary workers
* (less) wages and benefits saved during vacancy

Hiring costs include:
* cost of attracting applicants (agency, advertising, etc.)
* cost of screening applicants
* cost of interviews
* testing costs
* administrative, accounting and legal costs
* travel and moving expenses
* cost of medical exams

Training costs include:
* formal training costs
* other staff's time for on-the-job training
* salary during formal and informal training
* training of temporary/replacement staff
* cost of team integrating new member

Economic costs include:
* lost production during transition
* lost sales during transition

- lost intellectual capital
- lost or damaged relationships with customers
- cost of (re-)building relationships with customers and co-workers
- impacts on other employees (absenteeism, productivity, sick leave, etc.)
- impacts on suppliers
- cost of inefficiencies due to learning curve for new employee (12-13 months for employees to reach full efficiency)
- cost of inefficiencies due to departing employee

As turnover goes up, productivity per worker goes down. The Third Annual Industry Week Census of Manufacturers showed this trend by analyzing data from over 1,750 American manufacturing plants. Workers at plants with a turnover of less than 3% had almost 170% of the productivity of those at plants with a turnover of more than 20%.

Turnover	Productivity per Worker
Less than 3%	$200,000
3%-5%	$153,000
6%-10%	$150,000
11%-15%	$130,000
16%-20%	$125,000
More than 20%	$120,000

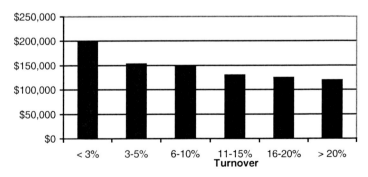

Productivity Per Worker as a Function of Turnover

22

Chapter 3 – Your Hard Costs of Stress

There is also a significant financial impact to turnover in the services sector. Employee turnover replacement costs have reduced earnings and stock prices by an average of 38% in specialty retail, call center services, high tech and fast food – four traditionally high turnover industries. It has also been shown for a retail stock brokerage firm that profitability would increase by two percent for every one- percent reduction in turnover.

In the 1980's, Rutgers University Graduate School of Management found that turnover costs averaged 120-200% of the salary of the position affected. This figure was updated by Bliss & Associates Ltd to 150% of compensation (salary *plus* benefits) for most employees, and to 200-250% of total compensation (salary plus benefits) for managers and sales professionals. This latter figure is included the StressCosts Formula™, as is the fact that 40% of these turnover costs is due to stress.

EAP Programs

Generally, for every dollar invested in an Employee Assistance Program (EAP) or an Employee and Family Assistance Program (EFAP), companies reap a savings of $7-$20 in increased productivity and morale, and a decrease in absenteeism, disability claims, and retraining costs.

Although personal stress and employee productivity are related, EAP interventions have been shown to improve productivity without reducing employee stress. EAP programs show no measurable impact on people with low to moderate levels of stress and only reduce stress in the short-term for those with high levels of stress. While they are effective, EAPs need to be part of a broader, more holistic strategy and are not, in and of themselves, sufficient to counter the effects of stressful work environments.

Different EAP providers categorize and measure their programs in different ways. While some organizations have reported that work and family stress account for as much as 75% of their EAP costs, a more conservative estimate of 55% has been included in the StressCosts Formula™ to reflect the findings of broader research. For a more accurate breakdown for your organization, consult your EAP provider.

Benefits

Significant research into the impact of stress on health care expenditures has been conducted with HERO, a large, multi-employer health promotion database. Individuals with self-reported, persistent depression (the most costly risk factor) had annual health care expenditures 70% greater than those who reported not being depressed. Those with the second most costly risk factor, uncontrolled stress, had annual adjusted medical costs 46% higher than those who were not stressed. Other risk factors such high blood glucose, hypertension, tobacco use and obesity lagged far behind these two leading risk factors.

Another HERO study showed that employees with modifiable health risks were responsible for 25% of total health care expenditures. Employees who were under constant stress with no methods for coping were responsible for 7.9% of total health costs. In contrast, being a former smoker and obesity were associated with 5.6% and 4.1% of total health care expenditures, respectively.

Between 1996 and 2001, Maritime Life Insurance Company reported a 43% increase in the number of short-term disability claims related to mental and nervous conditions for both white-collar and manufacturing occupations. In 1996 stress was the fifth most common reason for short-term disability, and in 2001 it was third.[1]

Across North America, stress-related disability accounts for 30% of disability claims (short-term and long-term disability). This number is the one used in the StressCosts Formula™.

Drug Costs

Anti-depressant and anti-anxiety prescription drugs are at the top of medical claims filed. In 2001, psychotherapeutic drugs accounted for 11.3% of prescriptions dispensed, and 9.8% of hospital and drug store purchases, growing 9.2% and 17.7%, respectively, over 2000 figures. Psychotherapeutics are second only to cardiovascular drugs. Analeptics, a particular type of psychotherapeutic drug, have been showing steady growth since 1993. The main analeptic product, methlphenidate, under the brand name Ritalin, has an average compound growth rate of 17.3% between 1993 and 2001.[2]

Chapter 3 – Your Hard Costs of Stress

The StressCosts Formula™ includes a conservative 10% of drug costs, which reflect the percentage of drug expenditures for psychotherapeutics. Stress is also a significant risk factor for cardiovascular disease. While cardiovascular drugs are the only segment larger than psychotherapeutics, there is no reliable information on how much of this can be attributed to stress, so they have not been included.

Workplace Accidents, Workers' Compensation Claims and Law Suits

While workplaces are much safer physically than they have ever been, occupational injury and illness numbers are increasing at epidemic proportions. These claims, according to Donald Millar, former Director of the National Institute for Occupational Safety and Health (NIOSH), are related to the "three modern occupational plagues" of cumulative trauma, indoor air problems, and job stress.

Job-related stress is a major predictor of "total work-related accidents," and workplaces that had high numbers of workers' compensation claims scored much more poorly on several factors including workload, personal life stressors, and job satisfaction. In a study at Boeing, workers who reported that they "hardly ever" enjoyed their job tasks were 2.5 times more likely to report a back injury than subjects who "almost always" enjoyed their job tasks. Organizations that have identified and addressed these deficiencies have reduced their workers compensation claims by as much as 81%.

Overall, 60-80% of workplace accidents are stress related, and workers with a more favorable working climate are less likely to experience accidents at work. Addressing worker psychology is now as important to preventing losses as engineering controls and safety training in manufacturing operations. The Traumatic Accident Model points out that stress is the root cause of injury and claims:

25

According to the Bureau of Labor Statistics, workers who had to take time off work due to stress, anxiety or related disorder were off the job for an average of 23 days (compared to 5 days for all non-fatal occupational injuries and illnesses). Nearly half of all occupational stress cases involved 31 or more days off, as compared with 19% of all occupational injuries and illnesses.

Nearly half of the states in the US allowed worker compensation claims for emotional disorders and disability due to stress on the job. In California, the number of Workers' compensation claims for mental stress increased by almost 700% over eight years, and ninety percent were successful with an average award of US$15,000. Courts in other countries are also recognizing cases like these as legitimate claims.

The StressCosts Formula™ uses a conservative 60% of the estimated total costs of all accidents in the workplace for the last year. For workers' compensation claims, the formula simply allows you to enter the total cost to your organization for workers' compensation claims, lawsuits, and associated costs.

Factors Not Included in the StressCosts Formula™

Because of the lack of solid numbers from research, there were some factors that were not included in the StressCosts Formula™. As mentioned above, absenteeism due to illness caused by stress and drug plan costs for stress-related illnesses (such as cardiovascular disease) was not included in the formula because there are no reliable percentages available from the research. Lost productivity due to stress and violence in the workplace is also not quantified by research.

Lost Productivity at Work

Marlin Company's 2001 Labor Day Survey showed that 82% of workers were at least a little bit stressed at work. Half say that they and their co-workers have more demands on them than a year ago, and 38% say they are feeling more pressure at work than a year ago. Generally, more individuals in larger organizations are stressed compared with smaller organizations.

Employee surveys from a range of American organizations show that 26-40% of employees report high levels of stress, and problems at work

were more strongly associated with health complaints than any other
life stressor, including financial or family problems. As many as one in
four employees view their job as the number one stressor in their lives,
and three-quarters of employees believe that workers have more on-the-
job stress than a generation ago.

In Canada, the 2002 Aventis Pharma Healthcare Survey found that half
of all employees with a health benefit plan face "a great deal of stress at
work," and that stress in the workplace has made one in four physically
ill at times. Forty-four per cent said that their employer didn't do
nearly enough to help them manage their workplace stress.

Data from the United Kingdom, shows that 15-20% of workers are
extremely stressed, 40-45% are moderately stressed and one in four
experience an illness caused or made worse by work. The Health and
Safety Executive (HSE) Survey of Work-Related Ill Health found a
30% increase in employees suffering from work-related stress over the
1990s.

In the European Union, approximately one in three employees reported
stress-related illness or health problems, and the Australian
Confederation of Trades Union has declared that stress is the single
most important health and safety issue. Given that workers from other
countries, such as Taiwan and Brazil, have been found to be more
stressed than people from the UK, stress is a problem that pervades the
entire industrialized world.

Despite the growing levels of stress in the workplace, there is no
established data that quantifies how much productivity is lost by
stressed workers in the workplace, so it has not been included in the
formula.

Violence in the Workplace

Violence in the workplace, including sexual harassment, ethnic
harassment, bullying, and physical violence, is escalating across the
industrialized world. Even though most cases of bullying and physical
violence still have a low profile because most cases are unreported, one
in ten employees still report working in an environment where physical
violence has occurred as a result of stress.

Workplace violence is actually greater in Canada than in the United States. One percent of American women reported being assaulted in the workplace, compared with 4% of Canadian women, and 4.2% of American men reported being assaulted in the workplace, compared with 5% of Canadian men. In the United States, however, 20 workers are murdered each week, making homicide the second-leading cause of workplace deaths, and the leading cause for women.

Forty-two percent of American employees work in environments where yelling and verbal abuse occur frequently, and almost one in three workers admit to yelling at workers because of workplace stress. Desk rage is a growing concern, and is fueled by a growing sense of helplessness with all the changes that are occurring in the workplace. Despite the fact that more women complain of on-the-job stress, men aged 25-45 years of age are most likely to explode with desk rage at work.

Between 1993 and 1998, the number of harassment cases reported to the US Equal Employment Opportunity Commission more than doubled, from 6,883 cases to 15, 618.   Over 40% of female American employees in the private sector, and as many as three-quarters of women in the United Kingdom experience sexual harassment at work. Ethnic harassment seems to have become subtler in some instances, replacing overtly racial jokes with more covert actions, such as excluding the individual.

Bullying occurs when one or more individuals persistently, over a period of time, are on the receiving end of negative actions from other worker(s), and are unable to defend himself against these actions. Being bullied has been linked with depression and anxiety, and people who are bullied are more likely to:

- make mistakes
- have accidents
- have lower job satisfaction
- have higher anger levels
- have higher stress levels

In fact, victims of severe bullying have been found to suffer from more serious symptoms of Post-Traumatic Stress Disorder than people involved in traumatic disasters, and in 1990, the cost of bullying to the organization was estimated at US$30,000-$100,000 per employee subjected to bullying. As many as 15% of employees are affected by bullying, and one in five employees have witnessed or been aware of verbal or physical bullying in their workplace.

While workplace violence affects nearly half the workforce, there are no quantitative findings that define its financial/ performance impact on the organization, so it has not been included in the StressCosts Formula™.

Using the StressCosts Formula ™

The StressCosts Formula™ is missing several components, and is extremely conservative in the figures that are entered. As a result, the number that you will derive will be an underestimate of the costs of stress for your organization. Despite this fact, it will likely be extremely large. You have to make a strategic decision with this number, against all your other financial figures. If one part of your organization was losing this amount of money, how long would you tolerate it? How much would you invest to stop the bleeding? This figure puts the nebulous concept of stress on the financial table so it can be put into its proper perspective, and so you can take appropriate action.

---

[1] Johnston B (2001) Stress leave way up, says Maritime Life Insurance, *The Daily News.* Sunday, October 7, 2001.
[2] IMS Health, Insights Into Health – Drug Monitor. www.imshealthcanada.com.

Chapter 4 – Understanding Stress

Stress is the body's response to any demand placed upon it to adapt. When you stress yourself, you catalyze 1,400 chemical and 30 hormonal changes in your body, some of which continue for *hours* after a stressful incident has passed. This was extremely useful when humans lived in caves and had to run from a saber-tooth tiger. Today there is nowhere to run, and the chemicals produced by chronic stress poison bodies rather than help them survive.

Dr. Hans Selye, known as "the Einstein of medicine," pioneered stress research in the 1930's and defined stress as the reaction that occurs when an individual's ability to adapt is overwhelmed by events. Stress is a subjective response, based on the individual's personality and physiology, and even small events or changes can serve to overwhelm an individual. Even 'positive' events, such as a promotion or marriage, that require an individual to adapt to change can produce stress. Selye defined two types of stress, distress and eustress.

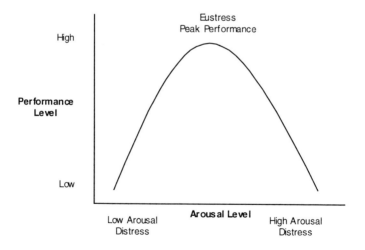

Distress, sometimes referred to as 'bad' stress, occurs when an individual experiences an overload of stress. This type of stress can occur when an individual is being forced into a situation, can't resolve a problem, doesn't have the resources to deal with the situation, and/or has little or no control over the situation.

Eustress is sometimes referred to as 'good' stress, and it is associated with situations where an individual feels challenged in a healthy way, has the resources to deal with these challenges, has some control and choices over her situation, and has sufficient rest between her challenges. Eustress is the effective use of stress by an athlete in a race, or someone working on a project that she is passionate about.

Theoretically, both low levels of arousal (resulting in boredom), and high levels of arousal produce both distress and poor performance, with optimal performance being achieved at an 'in-between' level of eustress. In practice, maintaining this balanced level is extremely challenging, and eustress easily turns into distress. What's more, while eustress can heighten performance for a particular project, constantly pushing an individual, without allowing sufficient time between challenges certainly leads to distress. An athlete cannot push 100% every day, and yet that is what organizations have been doing to their workers for decades.

What Happens When You Stress Yourself

Your autonomic nervous system is made up of two components, the parasympathetic system and the sympathetic system. Together, these systems regulate many of the processes in your body. With respect to stress, the parasympathetic system slows down the heart rate and reduces blood pressure, effectively calming your body, while the sympathetic system has the opposite effect. Both of these systems work together to keep you in balance under changing situations. Under stress, it's the sympathetic system that produces the 'fight or flight' response.

When a stressful event occurs outside of you, there are two routes that the information from your senses (sight, hearing, etc.) takes to the brain – a fast, direct route, and a longer, more circuitous route. The direct route goes to a small part of your brain called the amygdala. The other route is through your thalamus, which processes sensory cues, to the cortex, where information is analyzed to see if there really is danger or not.

Chapter 4 – Understanding Stress

The amygdala is the emotional center of your brain and acts as your early warning system. It's designed to produce a fast response, but not necessarily an accurate or an appropriate one, as it responds to cues which your brain has not yet analyzed. The amygdala is what produces startle reactions to sudden movements or surprises as it can instantly affect every system in your body to create the 'fight or flight' response. This sympathetic response includes increasing your heart rate, shutting down your digestion, and telling the adrenal glands to start pumping the stress hormone, cortisol, into the bloodstream. Epinephrine is also released, which increases your oxygen intake, speeds up your breathing, increases the blood flow, releases glucose, and dilates your pupils to prepare you for action.

In the meantime, on the other route, the same signal is being analyzed by the thalamus and cortex to properly assess the situation. If it is determined that there is no danger, then, *theoretically*, an 'all clear' is sent to the amygdala to stop the stress response, although this is not always so easily done.

Symptoms of stress include:

- increased heart rate
- elevated blood pressure
- shallow breathing
- headache
- change in sleep patterns (either sleeping too much or insomnia)
- change in eating patterns (either eating excessively or loss of appetite)
- irritability
- impatience
- aggressive behaviours (road rage, desk rage, etc.)
- depression
- listlessness
- restlessness
- withdrawal
- forgetfulness
- lack of concentration
- lack of self-esteem
- increase in smoking, and/or use of alcohol/drugs

The General Adaptation Syndrome

Hans Selye discovered human bodies are designed to maintain a state of balance, or homeostasis. When a stressor throws off that balance, the body adapts in an attempt to re-establish that balance. The process for re-establishing that balance is the General Adaptation Syndrome (GAS). Selye found that if that balance is not restored, and physical and emotional stress left untreated, always led to infection, disease, and eventually death.

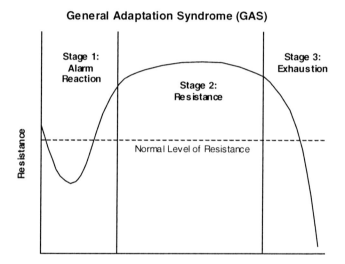

General Adaptation Syndrome (GAS)

The first stage of the GAS, the Alarm Reaction, is the immediate 'fight or flight' reaction to some external stressor. As part of this response, the immune system is depressed, lowering our resistance. If the stress passes quickly, the body returns to normal. Symptoms of this stage in the workplace include ongoing irritability, lack of concentration, and/or insomnia.

If the stressor continues, the GAS proceeds to the second stage, Resistance, which is where the body adapts to the stressor by releasing a variety of chemicals to boost the immune system. As a result, you can be lulled into a false sense of security and assume you are all right because you can actually become *more* resistant to illness and disease.

Chapter 4 – Understanding Stress

Unfortunately, your immune system is working above capacity to produce this resistance. If this stage continues indefinitely without sufficient breaks of rest and relaxation to balance off the stress response, you fall into distress and can fall prey to fatigue, procrastination, indecision, and other symptoms as you overuse and wear down your immune systems. This stage can lead to absenteeism, being late for work, and isolating yourself socially.

Finally, if nothing is done to rectify the situation, you run out of your physical, mental, emotional, and spiritual reserves, and your immunity collapses as you move into the final stage, Exhaustion. At this stage, organs begin to break down, adrenals are exhausted, and blood sugar levels collapse. At this stage, depression, physical and mental fatigue, and stress-related illnesses can all become chronic.

On a given project, eustress can potentially allow individuals to perform at an enhanced level. However, organizations have made a culture of working under constant pressure and this culture transforms eustress into distress. This constant pushing has been occurring for decades. Given the symptoms outlined in the previous chapter, it appears that a vast majority of the workforce is in the latter part of the Resistance stage of the GAS, or even moving into the final stage of Exhaustion, essentially at their breaking point. In trying to enhance performance, organizations have only succeeded in sabotaging performance, decreasing productivity, and increasing costs over the long-term.

Physical and Mental Health Effects of Stress

Stress, depression, and anxiety are related to changes in the numbers of white blood cells in circulation and natural killer cell activity. The longer the stress, the lower the number of specific types of white blood cells. In addition, typical symptoms of stress, including sleeping less, exercising less, poorer eating habits, increased smoking and increased use of alcohol and other drugs, all affect the immune system.

Cortisol, the stress hormone, is critical in small amounts to allow your immune system to function, and vital to the 'fight or flight' ability to run in the face of a threat. Chronically high levels of cortisol essentially act as a toxin in your body, and have been shown to:

- change the behaviour of certain organs
- cause arteriosclerosis (stiffening and hardening of arteries)
- impair immune function
- reduce glucose utilization
- increase bone loss and promote osteoporosis
- reduce muscle mass
- inhibit skin growth and regeneration
- increase fat accumulation (especially at the waist and hips)
- impair memory and learning and destroy brain cells
- be related to cancer

Negative mood states are linked with poor morale, absenteeism, and lower productivity. Stressed workers smoke more, eat more poorly, have more alcohol and drug-related problems, are less motivated on the job, have more trouble with co-workers, and suffer from more physical illnesses. In 2001, one-third of workers said that their jobs were harming their physical or emotional health and 42% said job pressures interfered with personal relationships.

Stress may contribute to the development of a wide range of physical and mental disorders including infectious diseases, chronic respiratory ailments, cardiovascular diseases, gastrointestinal disorders, depression and even cancer. Chronic job stress, resulting from a lack of control over work, can result in high blood pressure and trigger physical changes in the heart. The Journal of Occupational and Environmental Medicine reported that health care expenditures were nearly 50% greater for workers who reported high levels of stress.

Women who report high personal stress have greater odds of being diagnosed with arthritis, ulcers, asthma, back problems, chronic bronchitis or chronic emphysema. Men who report high stress have more of a chance of being diagnosed with arthritis, ulcers and migraines.

Stress can accelerate the development and growth of cancers without actually causing them. Research has shown that stress reduction strategies have prolonged life in cancer patients and have retarded tumors in laboratory animals.

Chapter 4 – Understanding Stress

Your diet also impacts stress significantly. Sugar, fat, alcohol, caffeine, the Pill and diuretics all interfere with the absorption of essential stress nutrients. Ironically, consumption of the first four increases significantly for many individuals experiencing stress.

Depression

A depressed mood involves having low energy and persistent feelings of helplessness and hopelessness. Depression is the single most common psychological condition treated by family physicians, and one in ten workers suffer from depression. It can be caused by job stress, a lack of fulfillment in one's career, or by a lack of empathy from managers.

The World Health Organization (WHO) has stated that
* depression will be the second leading cause of disability globally within the next 20 years, second only to heart disease
* five of the ten leading causes of disability are mental health or neurological problems
* fifteen percent of the world's population suffer from mental health disorders. This number increases to 40% when stress-related disorders are added in.

Bill Wilkerson, co-founder and CEO of the Global Business and Economic Roundtable said, "Depression is by far the leading cause of disability today… We are also seeing people today working harder and longer, but not more productively." A report developed by the Roundtable states that a key cause of stress is "a prolonged sense of constant catchup, interruption and distraction… Over time, such stress can trigger mental distress, which may further evolve to a medical condition among some."[1] The Roundtable estimates that depression costs the Canadian and US economies US$60 Billion each year, more than half of that in lost productivity.

80% of cases of depression can be successfully treated, making early detection and treatment critical. Currently only 6% of cases of depression are detected. If half of all cases were detected, it would save companies of 500 employees $10-15 Million in a five-year period, and companies of 1,000-10,000 employees could save $7-10 Billion in a similar time frame.

Stress Test – Measure the Impact of Stress on Your Health

The effects of stress are cumulative. The more changes you experience, the greater the impact on your coping mechanisms. In a classic study in the *Journal of Psychosomatic Research*, Dr. Thomas Holmes and Dr. Richard H. Rahe showed that a significant number of life changes (even positive changes) can lead to stress-related illness or accidents. The test below is based on this research.

To take this test, put a check mark next to each of the events listed below that you have experienced in the last 12 months. Beside each event is a number in parentheses. After you've checked off all the events that applied to you in the last year, total up the points next to each check mark to calculate your score.

___ (100) Death of a spouse

___ (73) Divorce

___ (65) Marital separation

___ (63) Death of a close family member

___ (63) Detention in jail or institution

___ (53) Major personal illness or injury

___ (50) Marriage

___ (47) Being fired from work

___ (45) Marital reconciliation

___ (45) Retirement

___ (44) Major change in the health/behaviour of a family member

___ (40) Pregnancy (self or spouse)

___ (40) Sexual difficulty

Chapter 4 – Understanding Stress

___ (39) Gaining new family member (birth, adoption, or remarriage)

___ (39) Major business readjustment (merger, reorganization, etc.)

___ (37) Major change in financial state (better or worse)

___ (37) Death of a close friend

___ (36) Change to a different line of work

___ (35) Major change in number of arguments with spouse

___ (31) Taking on a mortgage

___ (30) Foreclosure on a mortgage or loan

___ (29) Major change in responsibility at work

___ (29) Son or daughter leaving home

___ (29) In-law troubles

___ (28) Outstanding personal achievement

___ (26) Spouse begins or stops working outside of home

___ (25) Start or end formal schooling

___ (25) Major change in living conditions (rebuilding, remodeling)

___ (24) Change in personal habits (dress, manners, association, etc.)

___ (23) Troubles with superior/boss

___ (20) Change in residence

___ (20) Changing to a new school

___ (19) Major change in recreational habits (amount/type)

___ (19) Major change in religious or spiritual activities

___ (18) Major change in social activities

___ (17) Major new purchase (car, freezer, etc.)

___ (16) Major change in sleeping habits (a lot more or a lot less)

___ (15) Major change in number of family get-togethers

___ (15) Major change in eating habits

___ (13) Holidays/Vacation

___ (12) Christmas or similar holiday observance

___ (11) Minor violations of the law (traffic tickets, etc.)

Your Total Score:

Interpreting Your Score

Below 150
You have a relatively low level of life change, and your susceptibility to stress-related illness or accidents within the next two years is relatively low (35% chance or less).

151-300
You may be suffering from chronic stress, depending on your ability to deal effectively with the changes in your life. It would be advantageous to you to learn ways to deal more effectively with change and to minimize the adverse effects of stress. Your probability of a stress-related illness or accident in the next two years is approximately 50%. You may want to tap into resources to help you deal with the changes that you are facing.

Above 300
You are probably suffering from some of the detrimental effects of stress and should seek out resources to help you cope more effectively.

Chapter 4 – Understanding Stress

Some of the symptoms you may be experiencing include headaches, problems with sleeping (insomnia or sleeping too much), irritability, difficulty concentrating, depression, anxiety, difficulty balancing work and home, and indecision. You have an 80% chance of susceptibility to a stress-related illness or accident in the next 2 years.

Who's Impacted by Stress

White-collar workers, particularly in the lower levels of the organization and in the services sector, are most impacted by stress, and women are more likely to be adversely affected by stress than men are. While front-line employees show more visible symptoms of stress, such as absenteeism, there is evidence to suggest that managers and professionals also suffer from high levels of stress without such outlets. Mergers, downsizing, 'rightsizing' and ongoing technological changes have been significantly increasing the workload of the survivors of today's workforce. All of these factors have made it harder for people to maintain work-life balance, causing personal issues to impact on their performance at work.

Industry

Most of cases of occupational stress requiring days away from work were for white-collar workers. Half of all cases came from technical, sales, and administrative support occupations, and one in six came from managers and professionals. Health and social work employees are at the highest risk of prolonged absence due to occupational illnesses. Research also shows that, because of the intense schedules for product launches, IT professionals may also be experiencing especially high levels of stress.

The BLS Survey of Occupational Injuries and Illnesses revealed that the highest incidences of occupational stress occurred in services (35% of occupational stress cases), manufacturing (21% of occupational stress cases), and retail trade (14% of occupational stress cases). In the case of specific industries, finance, insurance, and real estate services showed a higher percentage of occupational stress cases than their percentage share of all workplace injuries and illnesses (12% versus 2%).

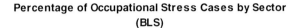

Percentage of Occupational Stress Cases by Sector (BLS)

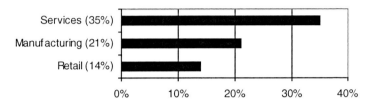

Research suggests that the stress level becomes more intense the higher you go in management. In fact, three-quarters of American workers said that they would *not* want their boss's job, and Gallup showed that most employees would rather be paid more in their current job than be promoted. The American dream has changed.

Demographic Factors

Women are more likely to report high stress than men. Generally, there is a decline in the reporting of high levels of stress as age increased for both men and women. Many more single parents reported high life stress than people who were unattached or part of a couple with children. Overall, as the education level of the individual rises, the level of work stress decreases slightly. The least educated group is twice as likely to report high life stress as university graduates.

Workload

In Japan, where there is an established track record of workers putting in long hours and dying in their most productive years from cardiovascular causes, there is a new term: *Karoshi*, which means "death by overwork." Since 1995, the United States has passed Japan in terms of hours worked and now the average American works a month longer each year than the average Japanese national, and three months more than Germans.

Although the average number of hours worked per week has not *appeared* to increase significantly in Canada since the mid-1960's, an 'hours polarization' has developed. The proportions of workers working both longer (41+) hours a week *and* shorter (less than 35)

42

workweeks have increased. One-third of Canadians aged 25-44 considered themselves to be workaholics, and more than half worry that they don't have enough time to spend with family and friends.

In the United Kingdom, full-time male employees worked 44 hours a week, compared with an average of 40 across Europe (39 hours in Germany), and 61% of employees in the UK work "sometimes" on a Saturday, compared to less than 40% in Germany. In Europe, despite being restricted to a maximum of 48 hours of work a week by health and safety rules, more than half of the 147 million workers in the European Union complained of having to work fast with tight deadlines.

Increasing competition, globalization and other factors have contributed to a great deal of downsizing, mergers and acquisitions, which are putting pressure on the remaining workers to do more work and to work longer hours, which is correlated with emotional exhaustion. Reorganization has been shown to significantly increase psychological distress and systolic blood pressure. Ironically, three-quarters of the 37,000 deals recorded by Thomson Financial Securities will fail to achieve the intended financial goals.

Uncertainty (about the job, future, etc.) contributed to these effects. The number of jobs lost in 1998 was greater than in any year in the preceding 50 years, and, over the 1990s, the number of workers who were afraid of losing their jobs more than doubled. Nearly half of all employees are worried about keeping their jobs.

More than half of all people who leave merged organizations do so because of merger-related stress. Seventy percent of the companies that had experienced downsizings and layoffs reported a substantial increase in disability claims, even with fewer employees. Union officials have reported that work force reductions may be linked to increased absenteeism, work conflict and grievances, and poorer supervisor-union member relations.

The 2001 National Work-Life Conflict Study suggests that life-long learning and career development remains simply propaganda, overall. It showed that the workers of today, the survivors of the organizational anorexia of the 1990s, have been with their organizations for nearly 14 years. However, the average time in their job was just over 7 years, showing little career mobility. Employees are working harder at the same jobs.

Overtime

Overtime, particularly unpaid overtime, has become an unhealthy expectation of many workplaces. Employees are dealing with reduced resources, increased competition, and one change after another. They are more insecure about their jobs, wanting to be seen as a contributor. As a result, many are afraid to refuse overtime, despite the impact on their personal lives and health.

Half of today's workers commonly skip lunch to complete their workload, and more than half have to work more than 12 hours a day to get their work done, donating an additional 18 hours of unpaid overtime to their employer every month. Overall, men, professionals, parents and employees with elder care responsibilities are more likely to work paid overtime, unpaid overtime, and to take work home.

Between 1991 and 2001, the number of employees taking work home increased from one in three to one in two employees. These employees spend an additional 6.7 hours of work working at home outside of regular hours, effectively donating an extra day of work a week to their employer.

Workers today spend more time on supplemental work at home and unpaid overtime than they do on paid overtime. Employees are more likely to work unpaid overtime than paid overtime (half of all employees work unpaid overtime, and one in three work paid overtime). Overall, managers and professionals are less likely to work paid overtime. Men in technical positions were both more likely to work paid overtime and to actually work more hours of paid overtime.

More than half of all workers don't feel comfortable refusing overtime. One in six said that they couldn't refuse it if asked, and 37% said they could only refuse overtime "sometimes." Non-professionals are afraid of losing their jobs if they turn down overtime, and professionals are worried that their career will stagnate if they don't work overtime or take work home

Chapter 4 – Understanding Stress

An additional impact on overtime, and a significant impact on work-life balance and stress, is work-related travel. Thirty-nine percent of employees work in jobs that required them to spend weeknights away from home, and one in four are required to spend weekend nights away from home. In addition to these numbers, one in three workers are required to spend time each week (an average of 17.2 hours a month on the road) commuting to a client site or to another work site. Men, managers and professionals are more likely to spend time away from home because of work.

The 2001 National Work-Life Conflict Study: Report One concluded, "the link between hours in work and role overload, work-life conflict, burnout and physical and mental health problems suggest that these workloads are not sustainable over the long term."

Organizations may *appear* to benefit from these added hours, but they are actually sabotaging their long-term performance. Individuals *can* perform at higher levels for short periods of time, provided they have some sense of control and appropriate rest between exertions. However, by creating a culture of perpetual crisis management, organizations are pushing workers into distress, and now are starting to reap the actual rewards of over-pushing their employees.

Work-Life Balance

While many individuals like to think that people have a personal life and a work life, the fact is that each person is one individual and has only *one* life. As such, stressors from their personal lives carry into work and vice-versa, and the challenge of balancing these demands adds to the pressure.

As much as many employers would like to separate work from personal issues, this separation cannot be done in practice. The fact is that inability to maintain the work-life balance has hard costs for the employer. "Work-life conflict occurs when the cumulative demands of… work and non-work roles are incompatible in some respect so that participation in one role is made more difficult by participation in the other role."[2] Such conflict affects the physical behaviours of workers (ex: eating and smoking habits), their mental health, and their physical health.

Marlin Company's 2001 Labor Day Survey provided further evidence
that both work and home caused stress in workers' lives:

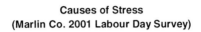

**Causes of Stress
(Marlin Co. 2001 Labour Day Survey)**

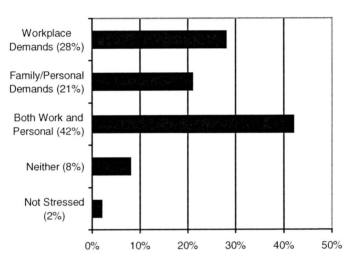

One third of workers find it increasingly difficult to balance work-life
responsibilities, and professionals are more likely than non-
professionals to report high levels of role overload. Generally,
employees with a high degree of work-family conflict and high levels
of interference in their family lives because of work:

- are less committed to the organization
- are less healthy, physically and mentally
- have higher job stress
- use more prescription drugs
- have higher usage of EAP/counseling services
- have more than double the absenteeism levels of employees with
  low levels of work-family conflict
- have lower job satisfaction
- have a higher intention to leave their jobs.

Chapter 4 – Understanding Stress

While men experience more interference in their family lives because of work, work longer hours overall, and have taken on more of the childcare burden, women are still primarily responsible for childcare, and responsible for most home chores. There is a significant body of research that suggests that women experience greater work-life conflict than men. It has not been clearly established whether this is due to biological differences, differences in socialization (ie: roles, etc.), or a combination of these factors.

A relatively new concern for workers is elder care. As many as 61% of workers have elder care responsibilities, and 13% have responsibility for the care of a disabled relative. More than half of those caring for elderly family members have to take time off from work to care for them. This new burden has also introduced a new sub-group, the 'sandwich generation,' which has both childcare and elder care responsibilities.

Parents and employees with elder care responsibilities work as many hours a week as employees without those responsibilities. Working parents have higher levels of work-life conflict and more interference in their work owing to their family lives than non-parents do, and employees with children are more likely to report high levels of job stress than employees without children.

There are also indications that Sick Building Syndrome (SBS) may not be solely due to environmental factors. Employees with higher levels of role overload and greater family support, but with lower organizational support, are more likely to report that their health had been adversely affected by their workplace. Although no direct link between workplace stress and SBS has yet been established, workers with higher levels of role conflict, role overload, and organizational stress, along with lower levels of organizational support, are more likely to report having poor air quality.

Alternative Work Arrangements

Flexible work hours have been shown to produce a wide range of benefits. Absenteeism and turnover rates drop, measures of job involvement and job satisfaction increase, and, indirectly, a reduction in overtime for unproductive work increases productivity. For the individual, role conflict is reduced, and mothers using flextime experience less behavioural depression.

While there has been a great deal of discussion about alternate work arrangements, few employers have implemented such arrangements. More than half of the respondents to the 2001 National Work-Life Conflict Study, work traditional, fixed hours. The breakdown of the use of alternative work arrangements, including flextime, compressed work weeks (CWW), and telework, is as follows:

Use of Alternative Work Arrangements
(2001 National Work-Life Conflict Study)

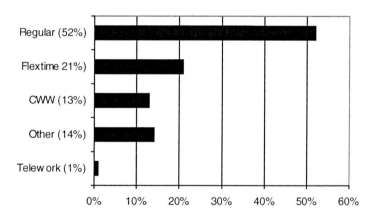

Flextime arrangements are more accessible to the private sector than the public sector, and managers and professionals are more likely to use flextime arrangements than non-professionals. Overall, though, those who have the greatest need for flexible work hours (parents and employees with elder care responsibilities) do not have access to them. Benefits of flexible arrangements such as improved attitudes and morale, improved ability to balance work and family, and increased productivity are proven. Despite this, claims by organizations of being 'family friendly' and 'employer of choice' remain largely rhetoric. Obviously there is still plenty of room for new strategies to be tested and implemented.

Chapter 4 – Understanding Stress

[1] Galt V (2000) Worker stress costing economy billions, panel warns. *Workopolis.com*, July 21, 2000. www.globeandmail.workopolis.com/servlet/News.
[2] Higgins C, Duxbury L (2002), The 2001 National Work-Life Conflict Study: Report One. Health Canada, p. 3. ISBN 0-662-32404-8.

Chapter 5 – What Causes Stress

Job demands and the amount of control an employee has are both related to the stress level and health of the employee. Even more important to reducing stress is the individual employee's coping ability and personal power. All of these are shaped and driven by the root causes of stress in the organization – the organization's systems, processes and culture.

Control, Coping and Reward

There are three relationships that stand out as predicting levels of employee stress and resulting physical and mental ill-health:

1. the relationship between the demands on the employee and the amount of control or influence he has over his or her actual daily work
2. the link between job demands and the coping ability of the employee
3. the correlation between the level of mental or physical effort an employee has to invest in reaching goals and the reward, compensation, or acknowledgement she receives for that effort.

Employees in high pressure/low control situations or high effort/low reward situations have much greater risks to their physical and mental well being.

In fact, high pressure, or "high demand" situations have already been identified as potential and actual occupational health and safety hazards in Canada.

Job Demands and Job Control

Control includes decision latitude, creativity, skills, task variety, and learning new things. Situations that are high in terms of what they demand of employees, and low in the amount of employee control over the situation, have significantly higher health risks than high pressure/high control and low pressure/low control situations. People in high demand/low control situations have:

- more than twice the rate of heart and cardiovascular problems
- significantly higher rates of psychological distress
- significantly higher rates of anxiety, depression and demoralization
- significantly higher levels of alcohol, and prescription and over-the counter drug use
- significantly higher susceptibility to a large number of infectious diseases

Workers with high levels of perceived control are not as likely to report high levels of conflict or interference between work and their family lives. The more control an employee feels over his own health and over things that happen to him at work, the less likely he is to report absences totaling six days or more in the previous year.

Control has been broken down into decision authority and opportunities for learning, the combination of which allows employees to learn and grow without significantly increasing their workload. Employees with high decision authority and high learning opportunities are healthier, more committed, more satisfied with their jobs, and have lower levels of stress.

Job strain is the measure of the balance between the psychological demands of the job and the amount of control or decision-making power it allows. Workers with high levels of job strain have been shown to have higher rates of a wide variety of diseases than similar individuals in low-strain jobs. One factor that can help people cope more effectively with job strain is having an integrated sense of one's life as being understandable, meaningful, and under an individual's ability to control it.

Support systems, both inside and outside the organization, are critical to helping workers deal with the negative effects of high strain jobs. Both the feeling of depersonalization and the negative effects of high strain jobs on job satisfaction were moderated with high levels of supervisor support. In addition, support from outside of the workplace, and support from co-workers for the employee reduced the negative effects of high strain jobs on job performance.

Chapter 5 – What Causes Stress

Job Demands and Coping Abilities

Coping, defined as expecting positive outcomes, considering problems as challenges and never being overwhelmed or resigned, has been found to have more impact on subjective health complaints than 'control'. People who have low coping abilities and who are in high demand situations reported more health complaints and job stress than all other groups, including high demand/low control groups.

Giving workers more control in their jobs is not enough. Increasing work control reduced the negative effects of stress only for individuals who believe in their ability to develop and implement a plan of action that will meet the demands of her situation. The outlook of the individual employee can be as important as the control she has in her job. This distinction is critical in understanding how and why individuals are able to deal with stress – or not.

Effort and Reward

Marlin Company's Seventh Annual Labor Day Survey showed that more than half of workers are not appropriately recognized and rewarded for good performance.

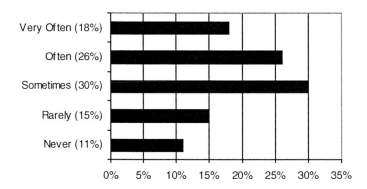

Receive Reward/Recognition for Good Performance (Marlin Co. 2001 Labor Day Survey)

Individuals in situations that require high levels of effort with low corresponding rewards, as compared with people in high effort/high reward situations, have:

- more than three times the rate of cardiovascular problems
- significantly higher rates of anxiety, depression, and conflict-related problems

When you add demand/control issues back into the picture, individuals experiencing a combination of high demand/low control and high effort/low reward have been shown to have:

- five times the rate of colorectal cancer
- three times the rate of reporting back pain, as compared with high demand/high control and high effort/high reward conditions
- as much as 150% greater incidents of repetitive strain injury (RSI)

Personal Power

These findings clearly show that the one predominant factor that determines the health of employees is personal power, which is the opposite of helplessness. Personal power is a combination of the employee's sense of confidence in being able to understand and develop a workable solution to the challenges he faces, his sense of meaning in what he is doing, and the employee expecting a positive outcome. Once these factors are met, having control over his job is important, and support from management, co-workers and home also have an impact.

Esther Orioli of Essi Systems conducted a study of 1500 employees in over 40 American and Canadian firms to explore the impact of different skills, beliefs and values, including self-care and relaxation. She found that only one factor predicted who would get sick and who would be healthy in work situations with high levels of pressure: personal power. Traditional stress management programs focused on self-care and relaxation skills, which only have a marginal impact on stress. That is why such programs have been proven to be ineffective in producing lasting results.

Cary Cooper, professor of organizational psychology and health at the University of Manchester Institute of Science and Technology in

Chapter 5 – What Causes Stress

England, supports Orioli's findings. He says that the most important work-related issue that research shows to be responsible for mental ill-health (and resulting absenteeism) is the level of autonomy and control people feel they have in their work and career development.

Health Canada identifies self-efficacy and social support as the key defenses to being overcome by stress. Self-efficacy is defined as "having a sense that you can influence the course of events in your normal daily life and that you can deal with their normal consequences. It also means feeling confident and sure of yourself."[1] By this definition, self-efficacy is, essentially, another term for personal power.

The top 10 sources of workplace stress, as identified by the Global Business and Economic Roundtable on Addiction and Mental Health, all contribute to reducing an employee's sense of personal power:

1. Too much or too little to do. The feeling of not contributing and having a lack of control.
2. Lack of two-way communication up and down.
3. Being unappreciated.
4. Inconsistent performance management processes. Employees get raises but no reviews or get positive evaluations, but are laid off afterward.
5. Career and job ambiguity. Things happen without the employee knowing why.
6. Unclear company direction and policies.
7. Mistrust. Vicious office politics disrupt positive behaviour.
8. Doubt. Employees aren't sure what is happening, where things are headed.
9. Random interruptions.
10. The treadmill syndrome. Too much to do at once, requiring the 24-hour workday.

The Systemic Roots of Stress
While an individual's personal power will determine whether or not he or she will be adversely affected by stress, the true roots of stress are not in the individual, but rather in the systems, processes and culture of the organization itself.

StressCosts Stress-Cures

Pascal Paoli, research manager of the European Foundation for the Improvement of Living and Working Conditions in Dublin, said that benefits programs address only symptoms. He stated that the sources of stress were in the organization's structure itself, the way work is organized and distributed, and in the levels of autonomy people have to manage their work.

The nature of many corporate cultures actually produces feelings and attitudes that make employees more liable to become ill, while organizations that actually empower and engage employees can literally reduce illness. W.L. Gore & Associates, a prime example of the latter, has health costs that are 29% lower than the national average.

One element of the corporate culture that shows up repeatedly in research is the impact of the management style. The management/leadership style and the culture of the organization significantly influence the personal power, and thus the stress perceived by the individual employee.

Cary Cooper identifies autocratic management, long working hours, and a glass ceiling for women as the root causes of stress. In his book *Work Rage*, Gerry Smith concurs, pointing out that management has, for a long time, been focused on results-driven skills, not people skills. The research clearly shows that supportive management helps reduce the negative effects of stress.

While a range of factors has been blamed for high turnover, there is a significant trend emerging in the research. The Saratoga Institute interviewed 20,000 workers who just left an employer and found that the number one reason for leaving was poor supervisory behaviour. A Gallup survey of 2 million workers at 700 companies confirmed these findings. Beverly Kaye, president of Career Systems International and co-author of *Love 'Em or Lose 'Em: Getting Good People to Stay*, says "People do not leave companies. They leave bosses".[2]

Employees who have less supportive managers are much more likely to cite the following reasons for thinking of leaving their jobs:[3]

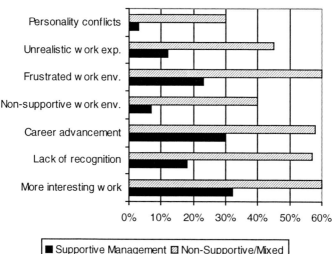

**Impact of Management Support on Reasons for Leaving
(2001 National Work-Life Conflict Study)**

More than one in three workers find it difficult at least sometimes to express their opinions or feelings about their job conditions to their supervisors and more than one in four employees rarely or never received appropriate recognition or rewards for good performance (only 30% "sometimes" receive appropriate recognition/rewards). Nearly one in three workers feel that their management isn't sufficiently sensitive to, or helpful in resolving the needs, conflicts or other problems that were stressful for employees.

The Impact of Supportive Management Practices
The 2001 National Work-Life Conflict Study asked respondents to rate their managers' performance on a number of behaviours. Supportive managers were those who performed well on a number of factors including effective communication, coaching, focus on output rather than hours, respect and consistency. Essentially, these are the characteristics of effective leadership. Non-supportive managers

exhibited the opposite behaviours, which are essentially characteristic of traditional, autocratic, command and control-style management.

Overall, employees who have managers who are more supportive are more committed, have much lower levels of job stress, and have higher job satisfaction than employees who don't receive such support. Employees who have supportive management are also less likely to report high burnout, less likely to report high depression, and much more likely to report having high life satisfaction.[4]

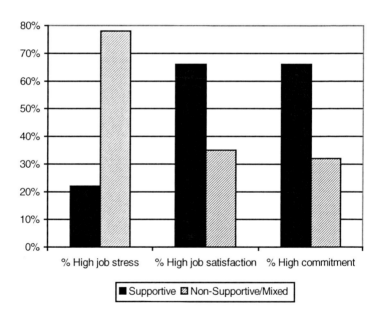

Impact of Management Support on Key Work Outcomes
(2001 National Work-Life Conflict Study)

Having a strong degree of role clarity (ie: knowing exactly what you need to do) *can* moderate the effects of a high workload, but *only* in situations where the employees had supportive leadership.[5]

Chapter 5 – What Causes Stress

Supportive management also impacts many of the critical factors in the StressCosts Formula™. As seen in the following graph, employees with supportive managers are less likely to take "mental health days" off.[6]

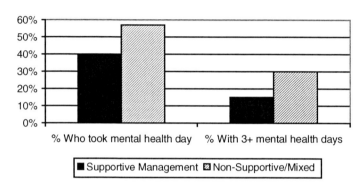

**Impact of Management Support on Absenteeism
(2001 National Work-Life Conflict Study)**

% Who took mental health day   % With 3+ mental health days

■ Supportive Management ▨ Non-Supportive/Mixed

Similarly, employees who have supportive managers are much less likely to purchase prescription medicine. This directly affects the bottom line of companies that offer drug plans.[7]

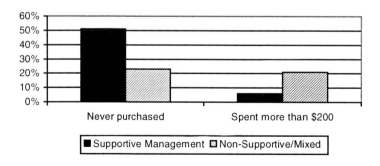

**Impact of Management Support on Prescription Purchases
(2001 National Work-Life Conflict Study)**

Never purchased   Spent more than $200

■ Supportive Management ▨ Non-Supportive/Mixed

The Aon Consulting Canada @ Work study showed that the top five drivers of commitment for Canadian workers were:

1) Management's recognition of work-life balance.
2) Opportunity for personal growth.
3) The organization's ability to satisfy customers' needs.
4) Competitive pay scale, consistent with industry standards.
5) Co-workers' skills keeping pace with the demands of their jobs.

It's interesting to note that pay comes in at number 4, well behind management's recognition of work-life balance. Also, this recognition of work-life balance refers to management's *active* recognition of the importance of personal and family life with policies, procedures and behaviours that enable employees to achieve work-life balance.

Management can support and enable workers to establish balance through a number of strategies, including:

- flexible work schedules
- personal time-off programs and career breaks
- job-share arrangements
- compressed work weeks
- telework/work-from-home
- competitive benefits
- training programs to help create work-life balance

Clearly, management style is directly linked to the impact of stress. The traditional management focus on results, and not on people, ultimately sabotages the original objective of increased productivity over the long run.

Job Satisfaction and Commitment

Many companies have made a direct connection between job satisfaction and profitability. MCI, for example, has found that satisfied employees are more effective and that a 5% drop in employee productivity cost them "a couple of hundred million dollars".[8] Job satisfaction has also been found to be the most significant factor for people who had a work-related accident leading to a disability claim.

Chapter 5 – What Causes Stress

The fourth annual Washington Business Group on Health/Watson Wyatt Worldwide survey on integrated disability management found that job dissatisfaction was one of the top five drivers of disability costs. "We consistently find that job dissatisfaction is a major factor affecting lost work days, which drives up disability costs," says Veronica Hellwig, a senior health and productivity consultant for Watson Wyatt. "Companies are missing a real opportunity to create a positive climate that engages employees so they want to return to work quickly."[9]

Organizations that offer a wide range of work-life benefits and that *aggressively* promote their use have the most satisfied employees. The most satisfied employees also have the lowest work-family conflicts, the lowest stress levels, and the fewest incidences of minor health problems.

MBAs, CAs, and law degrees are the qualifications for many of today's managers. Degrees such as these provide analytical training. Any training on actual leadership is generally more theoretical than practical. We train our managers to be number crunchers, and any actual leadership that emerges is despite this training, not because of it. Ironically, the focus on results and numbers has sabotaged the long-term viability and productivity of many organizations. It is only by focusing on people that the results are obtained. You manage things. You lead people. And the results of doing so drive the financial results.

---

[1] Best Advice on Stress Risk Management in the Workplace, Health Canada, Cat. No. H39-546/2000E, ISBN 0-662-29236-7, p. 6.

[2] Dobbs K (2001) Knowing How to Keep Your Best and Brightest. *Workforce*, April 2001.

[3] Higgins C, Duxbury L (2002), The 2001 National Work-Life Conflict Study: The Federal Public Service as an Employer: How Do You Stack Up? Power Point Presentation, Slides 58-59.

[4] Higgins C, Duxbury L (2002), The 2001 National Work-Life Conflict Study: The Federal Public Service as an Employer: How Do You Stack Up? Power Point Presentation, Slides 57, 62.

[5] Bliese PD, Castro CA (2000) Role clarity, work overload and organizational support: multilevel evidence of the importance of support. *Work & Stress*, 14(1): 65-73.

[6] Higgins C, Duxbury L (2002), The 2001 National Work-Life Conflict Study: The Federal Public Service as an Employer: How Do You Stack Up? Power Point Presentation, Slide 63.

[7] Higgins C, Duxbury L (2002), The 2001 National Work-Life Conflict Study: The Federal Public Service as an Employer: How Do You Stack Up? Power Point Presentation, Slide 61.

[8] Hiles D (1999) Friendly Workplaces. *Open Hearth*, Ohio State University Extension Office, April 4, 1999.

[9] Press Release (1999) Employer Efforts Can Pay Dividends in Reduced Disability Costs, Survey Says. Bethesda, MD, December 3, 1999. www.watsonwyatt.com/news/article.asp?ArticleID=6845.

Stress-Cures

Chapter 6 – How to Regain Productivity

Reducing stress and regaining productivity lost to stress can only be achieved by increasing the personal power of employees. There are two strategies to do this. The first focuses on the individual, and the second targets the root causes of stress – the systems, culture, and leadership style of the organization itself. Whatever action you take, it's critical to objectively measure where you start to establish a baseline, and to measure your progress against this baseline.

Individual Employee Strategies

Traditional stress and time management programs don't provide the skills employees need to deal effectively with stress. While employees who have good time management skills have improved symptoms of mental health, research has shown that there is little connection between the delivery of time management training and the regular use of time management skills. As identified earlier, traditional stress management programs focus on areas that have little impact on employees' ability to deal effectively with stress.

Today there are programs that have been proven to increase personal power. To ensure you achieve such increases, you have to measure what you want to change. Figures such as sick leave, absenteeism and turnover are relatively easy to obtain internally. You may be able to partner with your EAP or benefits plan providers to measure overall impact on those programs, while keeping individual usage patterns confidential. What's important is being clear on what needs to change, and measuring that, both before the program and afterwards.

Any program you introduce must enhance the personal power of employees and its impact must last long beyond the program itself. There are many surveys and instruments available to measure personal power, and other aspects of your organizational climate. A baseline measurement will determine where your people are before the program you initiate. Their progress after the training is measured against the baseline. Post-training measurements should continue well after the program ends to ensure lasting results.

All training programs must be evaluated to show that they provide a measurable change. Otherwise they're simply a cost, not an investment. Our own *Thriving In Chaos* Program, for example, has been shown to enhance personal power, to reduce absenteeism by 27%, and to significantly reduce the symptoms of mental and physical ill-health. We have done the research to substantiate these results.

Programs you bring in should be able to show a measurable impact, and effective program providers will work with you to measure the impact in your organization. Ask your provider for the evidence of their success, check out their references, and work with them to track your ROI.

The ROI of Wellness Programs

A review of workplace wellness programs around the globe found that, overall, they have an ROI of $1.95 to $3.75 per dollar invested. Canada Life launched a health-promotion program in 1978 and evaluated it over ten years to show a return of $6.85 for each dollar invested, based on increased productivity, reduced turnover, and decreased medical claims.[1]

The Journal of Applied Psychology reported on several studies conducted by St. Paul Fire and Marine Insurance Company on the effectiveness of stress prevention programs in hospital settings. One study showed that the frequency of medication errors halved after prevention activities were implemented in a 700 bed hospital. Another study showed that the number of malpractice claims in 22 hospitals that implemented stress prevention activities dropped by 70%. In comparison, 22 comparable hospitals that did not put in such programs showed no change in their number of claims.

A detailed study on the Union Pacific Railroad (UPRR) showed that UPRR could save as much as $77.4 Million in medical care cost increases over the decade following 1998 if it could implement effective risk factor modification programs. A decrease in the annual health risk of less than one-tenth of one percent would have more than paid for the health promotion budget.

Chapter 6 – How to Regain Productivity

These examples show that wellness programs have a solid ROI, *if* you're measuring the right things. Figures for absenteeism, turnover, and health costs are readily available. Some analysis is required to determine the impact of stress on these numbers, and the StressCosts Formula™ simplifies this process.

Working with individuals to enhance their personal power addresses the symptoms of stress. Addressing the root causes of stress is a much larger issue. The systems, processes, leadership and culture of your organization may be creating and perpetuating stress throughout your organization.

Cultural Systems

'Systems,' in this context, doesn't refer to the IT systems in the organization, but rather to the cultural systems – the inherent processes, procedures, and habits of doing business. Many of these are not explicitly written rules and policies. Rather, they are implicit ways of doing business that are aspects of the organizational culture.

Cultural systems are, at their core, cause-effect relationships that drive the behaviour in organizations. People learn how your organization operates – and how they are expected to behave – through these systems. These systems include the steps you need to go through to get approval for expenditures, your relationship with your boss, and your expectations for the amount of time that you need to put in at work.

You may find it challenging to see how these systems are creating your stress because they are "the way it's always been done." If it is your accepted way of doing things, you have rationalized exactly why it needs to be exactly the way it has always been. You've already bought into it because that's the way you behave every day.

If the response to failure is criticism and punishment by management, then employees learn not to go out of their way to do anything, and to spend their time protecting themselves and finding someone to blame. If management responds to failure by supporting the employee in solving the problem and in learning from their mistakes, then the organization will likely be more innovative and effective.

Systems can be used to simplify and make sense of work, but they can also cost the company in many ways. Let's say that company policy says that a customer cannot get a refund on a defective part, even if the company made the mistake. Even though the money will eventually be refunded to the customer by following an endless series of steps, that employee is helpless and receives the brunt of the reaction from that customer. This employee's personal power is compromised, their stress level increases and their productivity decreases.

The company may have brought in the policy because, at one point, the wrong decision was made, and management doesn't trust the employees to make the right decision. However, the resulting policy produces more customer dissatisfaction (and likely defection), and higher levels of employee helplessness and stress, which ultimately hurt the organization more than the original mistake. What's more, the hard costs of pushing the customer and employee through the process of reimbursement may cost the company much more than an incorrectly administered refund.

One of my clients was an organization that occasionally had to send people across a toll bridge to another facility. To ensure that nobody used company money for personal trips across the bridge there were several signatures required in order to get a bridge token. We added up all the costs (materials, salaries, gasoline, etc.) required to get these approvals, and found that it cost over $28 to ensure that an employee didn't abuse a 75¢ token.

Simple instances such as this one build on each other to create the organizational culture. These systems de-motivate and drain employees and produce hidden costs that cripple the organization. They have to be redesigned to support employees in producing the desired goals of the organization. This doesn't mean giving workers free reign and creating anarchy. It means controlling the right things, not everything.

Expectations of working overtime or of taking work home are parts of the culture of the organization that upset work-life balance, increase stress, and reduce overall productivity. The underlying causes of this institutionalized workaholism are all cultural:

Chapter 6 – How to Regain Productivity

- organizational anorexia due to downsizing and 'rightsizing'
- employees' fear of the negative consequences of "not being seen to be a contributor" by working long hours and taking work home
  - non-professionals afraid of losing their jobs if they turn down overtime
  - professionals worried that their career will stagnate if they don't work overtime or if they don't take work home
- hiring freezes and extended work hours to deal with different time zones due to global competition
- perpetual crisis management as a result of the speed of change and the organization's inability to plan and prioritize

These root causes are all dominant aspects of today's corporate culture that hamper employees' ability to maintain work-life balance, increase their stress levels, and decrease productivity. While these cultural habits may seem, on the surface, to enhance productivity, they ultimately harm it, and the organization, in the long term.

In the 1950's an American named Demming developed the concepts of statistical quality control that he said would improve production and profitability. The concept of zero defects seemed so outlandish and such a different way of thinking that North Americans all but ignored Demming. The Japanese and the Germans, who were struggling to rebuild their economies, however, did not, and their success soon left North American companies struggling to catch up.

One of Demming's core 'rules' was the 85/15 rule, which said that 85% of the problems in an organization came from its processes and 15% from the individuals and personalities. It is the processes and systems in an organization that are creating the stresses in the workplace. To truly eliminate the roots of stress and increase productivity, it is these elements that must be addressed. The challenge is seeing that the hard costs of stress are real, and not an outlandish concept as Demming's approach was initially perceived to be.

Symptoms of Stress-Inducing Corporate Culture
The following is a list of symptoms of cultures that produce stress. If you feel that more than 3 or 4 are applicable to your organization, then your corporate culture is producing stress and undermining your productivity. Or, more importantly, if your employees can, in a safe,

confidential, anonymous manner, identify 3 or 4 of these as being part of their daily existence, then you definitely are creating stress for them and hampering your effectiveness.

❑   high absenteeism
❑   high turnover
❑   high levels of short-term disability, long-term disability and stress leave
❑   people start each day with 25 or more e-mails (usually all marked urgent) and/or 25 or more voice mails (usually all marked urgent)
❑   overtime is routine and expected (working long hours, taking work home, travelling often)
❑   frequent reorganizations
❑   frequent changes in strategy
❑   people not taking vacations
❑   massive policy and procedures manuals
❑   high levels of union grievances
❑   last-minute reactions to competition (as opposed to innovating and leading the way)
❑   many committees, task-forces and study-groups
❑   managers spend most of their time in meetings in their own offices
❑   many massive control reports and documents
❑   employees can't state what the goals, vision and direction of the company are if asked
❑   few or no training opportunities
❑   people are busy studying issues, but doing/implementing little
❑   people are not having fun

Management and Corporate Culture

Work has changed significantly from the 9-to-5 workdays of a few decades ago to the 12-16 hour workdays (plus weekends) that are typical today. This change has evolved a little bit at a time, so it hasn't been immediately apparent. It's only when you look back over the last 30 years that the shift becomes clear.

There are many factors driving this evolution of work styles, including the increased focus on bottom-line results, and the lack of resources (people, money, time) that became the driving force of the "do more with less" mantra of the 1990s.

Chapter 6 – How to Regain Productivity

Demanding better results produced increased pressures. People can produce outstanding results under short-term pressure, but if that pressure is maintained, they simply can't keep up the same level of performance. By building that pressure day after day and creating a crisis mentality, organizations created today's massive costs, as detailed in the StressCosts Formula™.

This, however, is not the 'fault' of the managers who focus solely on results. Much of this comes from their training. As stated before, managers often have a law degree, an MBA, or a CA, all of which teach how to analyze and work with concepts, but not how to be a leader. Of all the persistently good companies Jim Collins studied in his book, *Good to Great*, only one was led by a CEO who had an MBA.

Effective, supportive leadership is what is needed to build the cultural systems that produce lasting, growing results. Leadership can't be learned in a classroom or a textbook. It is learned in the field under the guidance of an effective mentor or coach. Unfortunately, most people are left to their own devices, or expected to know how to lead intuitively because they're in a leadership position. And like the Emperor and his new clothes, many of these people are afraid to admit that they don't know, because they feel they are expected to know how to lead.

Examining and redesigning your organization's leadership and systems is not a task that can be passed on to the lower levels – it has to be executed from the top down. It requires objectively evaluating the *entire* organization to identify what is working effectively, and what is creating stress and interfering with productivity.

How Management Style Shapes Organizational Culture
Robert J. Danzig rose from being an office boy for the Albany Times Union to becoming that newspaper's publisher 19 years later. He then became President of the Hearst Corporation's newspaper division for 20 years and, in that time, increased cash flow one hundred times from what it was when he began.

Danzig's success comes from three core philosophies. First, seek out and nurture the best talent. Second, be in the habit of celebrating all the

achievements of your people, because they are the ones who produce
the results. Third, be strategic, not operational. He firmly believes that
successful leadership is about being a leader, not a manager, and that
leadership is about finding the noble purpose of your business and
realizing that vision.

His values were seen in his day-to-day actions. When he was President
of the entire newspaper division of the Hearst Corporation, whenever
he was in his office and not travelling, his assistant would send out a
notice to the managers across the division. By 4pm that day, each
manager was to have key information to him about one person who had
done something worth celebrating. They were to send Danzig that
person's name, his or her spouse's name, the employee's home address,
and one sentence outlining what the employee had done for the
company.

Each of those people would then receive a note from Danzig thanking
the employee for what she or he had done for the company. These
were not cards that he signed en masse, or that were stamped with his
signature. These were hand-written notes from him on his personal
stationery. Danzig then wrote a note to the employee's spouse
congratulating him or her on the good news, and sent this along with an
appropriate gift for the spouse. Thus, the spouses asked the employees
what this was about and the employees had a chance to restate their
achievement and to celebrate again at home.

After leaving Hearst to launch a new career as a professional speaker
and author, Danzig visited his successor and was surprised to find out
that he was continuing this tradition. By way of explanation, his
successor, who had been with the chain since 1979, pulled out every
letter Danzig had sent him. This practice of recognizing employees'
accomplishments was now firmly entrenched in Hearst's culture.

Danzig stated that he made a *habit* of celebrating all achievements, not
just the big ones. His notes are wonderful feedback, yet if he had
written the notes and been in the habit of being neutral, or even critical
to his people outside of this action, it wouldn't have had the same
impact. He had to have been consistent in his behaviour in *all* that he
did, and that made it relevant for his managers to emulate him. Only
by being consistent in living his values did he transform the culture of

the organization, and it's little wonder that he produced the outstanding financial results that he did. His actions built the systems that enhanced the personal power of his people, and thus freed them to produce the results he needed.

Measurement Systems

Measurement is critical in making effective changes to organizational culture and systems. In addition to the HR measures and personal power, it's critical to take abstract concepts such as 'satisfaction,' 'leadership,' and 'culture,' and put hard numbers to them. There are several proven climate and leadership surveys that very effectively quantify what were previously considered to be abstract concepts. Make sure you talk to people who have used the survey instrument you're thinking of using to ensure that it is a practical and useful tool.

The first measurement you take acts as a baseline and as a diagnostic tool. It will identify your strengths and the areas you need to improve, which will help define your action plan. When you redo the survey in a year, you will be able to see exactly how you have improved. These numbers need to be as important – or even more important – than your financial results because these numbers drive your financial results.

This type of approach affects the organization as a whole, including the top leadership. It is often useful to have a proven consultant working with you to provide an objective and more neutral perspective, and to guide the process. In selecting a consulting organization, interview several organizations that have worked with the consultants. Ensure that the consultants help to deliver quantifiable and lasting results to their clients. Once again, consulting services are an investment and you deserve a return on your investment.

In addition to the softer issues that are measured with a climate and leadership survey, HR elements also need to be measured, as you would in the first strategy in this chapter which targeted individual employees. Of course, you must also track overall performance measures. All of these will be used to calculate the overall impact of this initiative to your organization.

Targeting the culture and leadership of your organization involves a great deal of analysis, individual reflection, and work. It will generally take at least two years to create a cultural shift that will last. However, the financial payback for such an initiative can be phenomenal.

The ROI of Effective Management Practices

Frank Russell Co. prepared an index for the 1998 "Fortune 100 Best Companies to Work For" and compared its performance with the Standard and Poor's (S&P) 500 for the same time frame.

Financial Performance of the Fortune 100 Best Companies to Work For

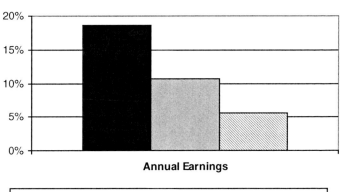

Assuming a market-cap-weighted index, S&P showed annual earnings of 5.7%, while the Fortune 100 Best index scored 10.6% annually. If the stocks were each weighed equally, the Fortune 100 Best index would have shown an 18.6% annual growth. At the top of the 1998 Fortune list was Southwest Airlines, which has been recognized repeatedly for their supportive management practices. Financially, Southwest provided a 26% annual return over the previous four years in an industry that has been struggling for years.

Dennis Kravetz has developed an index, called the PMP score, for rating an organization's people management practices (PMP). He tracked firms with both high and low PMP scores over 10 years, and found that organizations that have good people management practices reduce, or even eliminate, many workplace stressors. The results also show in their sales growth, profit growth, profit margin, earnings growth and ROI. The figures in the following table and graph are the annualized results of ten years of data.[2]

Financial Factor	Companies with High PMP Scores	Companies with Low PMP Scores
Annual Sales Growth	**16.1%**	**7.4%**
Annual Profit Growth	**18.2%**	**4.4%**
Annual Profit Margin	**6.4%**	**3.3%**
Annual Growth (earnings/share)	**10.7%**	**4.7%**
Total Annual Return (stock appreciation + dividends)	**19%**	**8.8%**

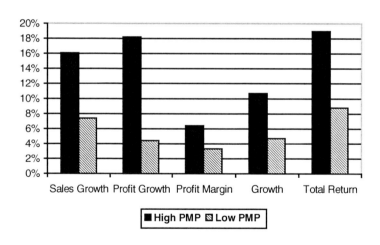

Financial Performance of Effective People Management Practices

Kravetz also found that, of the 20 companies that had the highest PMP scores in 1987, 80% were still in business in 1996. Of the 20 companies with the lowest PMP scores in 1987, only 30% were still in existence 10 years later.

Watson Wyatt's Human Capital Index™ (HCI) measures 30 key human resource practices for finding, developing, supporting and rewarding human capital in organizations. The HCI was compared to financial measures of a company's value. In North America, the total returns to shareholders of high-HCI companies averaged 70%, medium-HCI companies 20%, and low-HCI companies –6%. Similar results were obtained in Europe as well.

Return to Shareholders for Effective Human Resource Practices

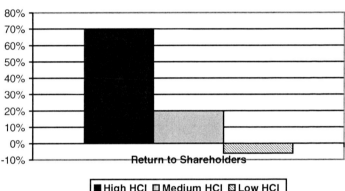

Simply put, stress has hard costs for all organizations, and effective, supportive management has solid, bottom line payback. It makes simple business sense to refine the culture and leadership of the organization to recover productivity lost to stress – and to enhance productivity even further. Until now, the organizational culture, leadership, and productivity have been talked about, but rarely focused on because they weren't effectively measured. Now the tools exist to measure all of these factors and to make a lasting, positive impact on both your people and your bottom line. One leads to the other.

---

[1] Dyck D (1999) The Wellness Package. *Benefits Canada*, January 1999.

---

[2] Kravetz DJ (1996) People Management Practices and Financial Success: A Ten-Year Study. www.kravetz.com.

Chapter 7 – Building Systems That Work

Systems are nature's way of keeping things in balance. They are the way all of nature works, including the systems of people in organizations. Engineers incorporate systems thinking for effective design and, over the past several years, so have effective businesses. Whether your business is successful or struggling, the behaviours that create your success or struggle are driven by your systems. By designing effective systems, you create effective organizations.

In order to understand how systems work, let's look at how the following system is used in a simple example.

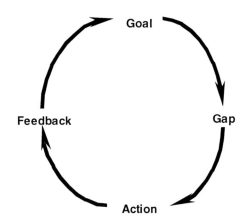

Let's say you want to heat a room that's at 15° Centigrade to 20°. Your *Goal* is 20°, and the *Gap* is +5°. The *Action* that the heating system takes is to turn on the heat. The *Feedback* is the rising temperature in the room. If the temperature goes up to 22°, then the *Gap* is now -2°, and the *Action* taken is to shut off the heat, and so on. Once you set the thermostat, it takes care of all of these changes. All you have to do is set the goal, and this system makes all the changes you need to keep things in balance at your desired temperature. That's a heating system.

Your stress response works in much the same manner. As explained in Chapter 4, your autonomic nervous system is made up of the parasympathetic nervous system and the sympathetic nervous system. At the simplest level, the *Goal* of this total system is to keep you safe and healthy. In the event of something startling you, the *Gap* is that you are in danger, and your sympathetic nervous system takes the Action of triggering your fight or flight response. The *Feedback* is what happens as a result of this. If you remain in danger, the *Goal* of health and safety has not been met, maintaining the *Gap*, and maintaining the same *Action* (the stress response). If, however, you have moved out of danger, and are now safe, the increased chemicals pumping through your system are not healthy, producing a different *Gap*. In response to this, your parasympathetic nervous system takes *Action* to calm your body and restore balance. This entire system runs on its own, without your conscious involvement.

Core Cultural System for Organizations

In an organization, an effective system has six key elements: the vision, the values, the goals, relevance, feedback and action. These elements interact as shown below.

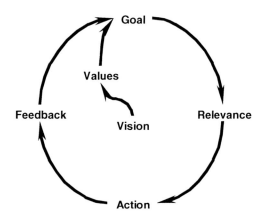

Chapter 7 – Building Systems That Work

We will examine how each element works individually, and how this system can increase or decrease stress. At the end of this chapter, and in the next chapter, in interviews with leaders who create systems that enhance personal power, you will see how these systems translate into actual workable solutions.

How Systems Drive Behaviour

Example 1

A friend of mine joined an organization that said that it looked after its people and supported balanced lives and healthy families. My friend wanted to be home with family by 5:30, and was assured that was fine. Once on the job, it turned out that everyone worked 12-16 hours a day, 6-7 days a week. Every day started with 40-50 e-mails, all marked urgent, and 40-50 voice mails, all urgent, and each and every day was spent fire-fighting. It was impossible to complete the workload in less than 12 hours a day. Within a few weeks, my friend was at a crossroads – to be carried along with the whirlwind, or to leave, and was fortunate enough to choose the latter.

That organization had two sets of values and acceptable behaviours: those that were stated, and those that were actually practiced. The actual values translated into working long hours, which was out of alignment with my friend's goals. The peer pressure of everyone working those long hours was one way that the organizational culture forced its way into new employees, and often carried them along before they knew what happened. It created relevance to the goal of long hours. There was little actual feedback because the manager was too busy, so the only feedback was the backlog of voice mails and e-mails, which also supported the need for long hours.

Ironically, with all the busy-ness, there often wasn't a great deal being done. The value was 'busyness,' which was expressed by making sure you were busy doing some activity, not necessarily producing results. As a result, everyone was busy responding to e-mails and voice mails, having meetings, making power point presentations, and being far less productive than they could have in a more sane work day.

Example 2

Many organizations say they are looking for innovation to find better ways of doing things, yet provide feedback that gives the opposite message. The problem is, when they think of innovation, most of them only see the successful innovations and the payback that they provide. The fact is that if you encourage innovation, there is one and only one thing that you are guaranteed more of: failure. Not all innovations succeed on the first try – in fact, few do. It is continued application and resolving the 'failures' and problems that produces the final innovation.

Thus, the amount of innovation you have in your organization will be driven by how you deal with failure. If the feedback you provide is to punish failure or penalize people for not attaining their goals when they try something new, then you kill innovation. That type of feedback changes the goal relevance to your employees. They are then focused on protecting themselves from being penalized, taking no chances or initiatives, and playing it safe.

If, on the other hand, your feedback is to support failure, as effective leaders do, by asking, "what have we learned from this? How do we resolve it and move forward?" then you will likely have more innovation, including those that pay off ten-fold to more than make up for all of the 'failures.'

Example 3

A bank realized customers were frustrated or annoyed by simple banking problems in dealing with tellers. The tellers had to move the problem up to management to resolve these issues. The cost in the managers' time and in lost business was staggering. Thus, this bank brought in a policy that any teller could spend up to $100 without authorization to solve any customer's problem.

Despite this initiative, few tellers did anything. The problem was that, for years, the feedback tellers had received was to be reprimanded for doing anything out of the ordinary for their customers, deteriorating their personal power. As with the innovation example, above, their most relevant goal became self-protection, so the tellers learned to do nothing extra. Simply giving them the power wasn't enough to break the inertia of the past. They could learn to take the initiative the bank wanted, but it would take a great deal of coaching and supportive feedback for their smallest actions to convince them that it was safe to take a chance.

Their supervisors needed to have the time to coach the tellers, and that was a challenge because the cultural systems that drove *their* behaviour gave them no time. Because of the bureaucracy involved, these supervisors spent most of their time in their offices doing paperwork. Those goals had been made relevant by the bank. Thus, while they wanted to help the tellers, they were held accountable for producing reports the bank wanted, and so were not able to produce the results required with the tellers to enhance customer satisfaction. Customer satisfaction was important, but not as important (relevant) as the reports.

Example 4

Probably the most mind-numbingly-inane system that pervades the public sector around the world is the fact that, if a manager doesn't use his entire budget, that budget will be reduced by that amount the next year. Because of this feedback, just before fiscal year-end, it's like Christmas again, as everyone desperately tries to spend all their money so that they won't get less next year. In an age where fiscal responsibility is urgently required, many governments are encouraging their people to spend without reason. The relevant goal is to not lose budget for the next year. There is no reward for fiscal responsibility, only for fiscal irresponsibility, and so costs continue to spiral upward unchecked.

Vision

Your organization's vision provides the focus for all your people to ensure that each one is acting and making decisions in the best interests of the organization. Without this understanding, an employee may make what she believes to be the best decision, from her limited perspective, but which may cost the organization far more in the long-term.

You can sculpt a vision at several levels, as illustrated in the Value-Added Curve, below. The axis along the bottom shows the needs of the employee that are met by the organization, ranging from physical needs through informational and so forth. The vertical axis shows the value added to the employee, and also the corresponding value the employee re-invests into the organization as a result of that level of organizational commitment.

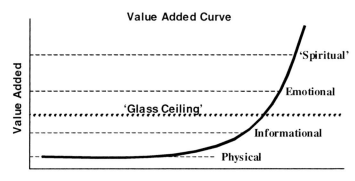

Value Added Curve

Value Added

'Spiritual'

Emotional

'Glass Ceiling'

Informational

Physical

Employee Needs Met by Organziation

Meeting the physical needs of the employees means that they are told what to do in their corner of the world, and expected to do it in exchange for a paycheck. Ideally, employees have the resources they need to do the job. In reality this ideal is rarely the case. At this level, employees are in the dark as to what is going on elsewhere in the organization, have no idea of what the vision is (and there may not be one) and may not even be clear as to what the organization does overall. Employees can easily do something that hurts the organization overall because they don't know any better, and they are often severely punished or reprimanded if that happens.

At this level, personal power can be extremely low, and thus the costs of stress extremely high. This drop in personal power is exacerbated when there are many organizational changes. These changes are demanded without any reason being given, increasing feelings of helplessness. One of the reasons such information is withheld from employees is the traditional view of information being power. Managers withhold information because they perceive that doing so gives them power.

I have seen organizations at this level actually get employees motivated enough to work together to solve a problem. When one such team

84

made the presentation to its CEO, he applauded them for their work, and then said that it was good considering what they knew, but there was one additional piece of information they didn't have that invalidated all of their work. He knew that piece of information before the team started, but he kept it to himself. In so doing, he was worse off than before. He actually got them working together on a problem – this time. The next time, they'll have nothing to do with it. What's the point?

The next level of employee needs that can be met are their informational needs. This level involves letting them understand how they fit in the organization, what the organizational goals are, and how it is doing. Employees understand how they fit in the puzzle and how they contribute, allowing them to make more effective decisions.

At the informational level, employees' personal power is enhanced, and they are more likely to make decisions that support the organization. The costs of stress will likely be lower and the employees are more likely to perform consistently at a satisfactory level. However, to consistently perform at a high standard, they need more.

It is only at the emotional level that vision starts to take root. While it has to be kept simple, an effective vision has to be compelling to all employees. There must be an emotional buy-in that compels each employee to commit to a higher level. That is why there is a 'glass ceiling' between the informational and the emotional level. It is at this level that the difference between managing things and leading people becomes clear. This level on the Value-Added Curve is where leadership is required throughout the organization to build the personal power and tap the full potential of each employee in the organization.

A true vision addresses the spiritual need of the employee to be a part of something greater than one person alone. It means having a vision and a purpose that are so compelling that people want to be a part of it and a part of creating it. It is this level of commitment that creates the scores of legendary stories common to organizations such as Federal Express, where drivers pawned their watches to buy gas for their vehicles. These people were part of something greater and, because they were, their levels of commitment went through the roof.

When the Gulf War hit, the entire Department of National Defense worked together at a level that hadn't been seen in years. They broke every rule in the book, all union-management issues were tossed aside, and they were operational in three weeks because they had something greater to which they were all committed. In wartime, they have a common focus and a clear and compelling vision, but in peacetime, there is no such common driving force for them, and all sorts of problems and bureaucracy get in the way.

As challenging as it is to create a compelling vision, just having it by itself is not enough, as evidenced by the military. Their systems do not support working together effectively over the long term. Like any bureaucracy, they drive organizations down to addressing only the physical needs of the employees – or worse. The Gulf War created a compelling vision and urgency that over-rode those systems. However, once the urgency abated, the bureaucratic systems reasserted themselves and the traditional problems resurfaced. Each element in this system is critical for long-term results. The vision is a starting point, but is useless without the other elements of the system in place to support it.

Values

High performing organizations are clear about their values and about how these values translate into day-to-day behaviours. They use their values strategically, to guide every decision and action. However, for most organizations, values statements are simply rhetoric that sits on a fancy plaque on the wall. Your real values are seen in the halls, not on the walls.

Values are usually single words (such as 'success,' 'trust,' 'teamwork,' etc.) or short phrases that have a great deal of emotional power for the individual or the organization that lives by them. They define what is acceptable behaviour and what is not. Values are the non-compromisable rules of the game that, when violated, stop all action.

While your vision shows where you are going, your values describe how you are taking the journey. The challenge with values is that they are vague concepts that mean different things to different people. Each person generally has a strong sense of what common values (trust, hard-work, etc.) mean, but the definitions different people have for the same value are usually different.

Most people, for example, may say they have integrity. If you ask them, you'll find that the internal definition that each one has is unique. To one person, integrity may mean being truthful, while to another, it may mean doing what you said you would do. Thus, while two people may seem to agree on the concept, they may come into conflict when it comes time to put that value into practice in day-to-day action.

Instead of just stating abstract value statements, each value needs to be translated into the behaviours that it would drive, so that everyone is clear on what they mean. The meaning of each general value needs to be interpreted in a way that everyone can understand and agree upon. They then have to be used and lived by.

There are two types of organizations. First are those that clearly spell out their values and what they mean in terms of expected actions, and then use these values strategically. Then there are those that may make values statements, but when the crunch comes, these values are abandoned because the organization has to make business decisions in the 'real' world. Ironically, the financial results of the first type of organization are often orders of magnitude better than the latter.

If you don't live the stated values, you essentially have two sets of values – those that are actually lived and which form the basis of the organizational culture, and those that are stated as the ideal but which are not rewarded or supported. Organizations putting value statements on the walls that are not seen in the halls are simply seen as being hypocritical by their own people. Employees can't trust what's said, and so live in greater uncertainty, impairing their personal power and increasing their stress levels.

Your actual organizational values, and the associated acceptable behaviours, and thus your organizational culture, come from management – from the C.E.O. down – in two ways. First, their actions model the desired and expected behaviours. The second way lies in what they expect from those who report to them. In an effective organization, these two will be the same. In less effective organizations, what management asks of its people is different from what they do, and that, in itself, is a behaviour that is passed down. If the C.E.O. says one thing and asks another, then so will management all the way down the line.

Accountability is critical when it comes to using values strategically. To truly give people a sense of control over their environment, you have to be able to hold everyone – including the C.E.O. and senior management – accountable for living the values. It must be safe for *any* employee to call *any* employee or manager on it when he is not living the values. This freedom to challenge anyone in the organization is the true test of whether or not an organization is living its values, or not.

One other issue to be considered with respect to values is that the values of the individual employees must be aligned with the organizational values. If they aren't, that doesn't mean that the organization or the individuals are 'bad' – they are simply different, and they don't fit together. I've had some amazing people working for me. I respected them deeply and recognized the incredible potential each of them had. Unfortunately, in some cases, it simply didn't work out because the values of my company and their personal values didn't fit together, so they couldn't do what was required of them here. They were very good, capable people – with different priorities. So this wasn't the place for them.

Goals

In a simple system, like the thermostat mentioned above, it's enough to state a goal. In an organization, the goals of all the stakeholders have to be aligned, so that everyone wins and you're moving in the same direction, instead of fighting against each other. The goals translate the vision and values into objectives. Aligning the goals makes sure the employees are moving in the same direction as the organization.

An organization's success (profits in a for-profit company, and operating within budget for the public sector) comes from meeting or exceeding the customer's goals, whether you're dealing with a customer internal to your organization or an external customer. The challenge comes from those times when you can do the extra things that make a difference or when you have to deal with problems that arise. Unfortunately, whenever these "moments of truth" arise, management is hardly ever there. It's usually the front-line person, and she is rarely motivated by the systems to do those extra 'little' things. In fact, in most organizations employees are usually motivated to get in the way of or annoy the customer.

Let's look at a simple example. I was in a drug store buying an 85¢-candy bar. The clerk made a mistake and had to wait for the front-store manager to come from the back to void the cash register. The manager thought he had made a bright decision hiring this kid at basic wages, and that the kid should have been grateful to have a job because so many kids were looking for work. The problem was that, by not trusting the kid to correct an 85¢ error, the kid was basically told that he was neither trusted nor respected. The clerk was demeaned. Nothing motivated him to even smile at me or apologize to keep me from getting annoyed – which *might* have prevented me from taking all my future business elsewhere. The manager made a sale, and lost a customer, which kills profits. The clerk's personal power and commitment to the organization weren't even measurable, and turnover was probably high, all of which sucked away at the financial health of the store.

Freeing people to help the customer doesn't just apply to kids working part-time. Most organizations limit the abilities of front-liners to handle issues with the customer. Either these employees can do nothing, or they have to go through so much red tape and paperwork that they frustrate and annoy the customer. And then a supervisor or manager comes along and easily does what the front-liner is fully capable of doing, but not allowed to do. And if the front-liner does something out of the ordinary to help a customer, he is usually told off. Systems such as this may seem simple and harmless, but in actuality they tear personal power to shreds, increase stress on the employee, and reduce productivity.

If employees are concerned about their supervisors getting upset with them for making mistakes, they will spend all of their time playing it safe, covering up and shifting blame. Their primary goal will be self-protection, which once again hurts the organization because it builds in inefficiencies and erodes personal power.

If the main treatment front-line employees receive is criticism for mistakes, they generally care little about the company or the people it serves. Unfortunately, that employee, to many customers *is* your organization. If these employees are that helpless and stressed and uncaring, that is how the organization looks to its customers. In reality, such treatment is not only applicable to front-line staff. Hampering people from doing their work happens at all levels in the organization, with similar results. When a manager's hands are tied, the constraints multiply down to all the people who report to him.

There is a simple concept that enables you to examine how well-aligned the goals are in your organization: C.E.O. Goals. In this case, C.E.O. stands for something quite different from the normal usage. It stands for:

Customer
Employee
Organization

This doesn't mean that these goals need to be the same – they simply have to be aligned.

The organizational success (profitability or operating within prescribed budget) comes from meeting or exceeding the needs of the customer. The challenge is in aligning the goals of employees at all levels of the organization with this need to meet or exceed customer needs. What are the systems driving the employees? Are the employees constrained to lead the customer through a quicksand of red tape to deal with a simple issue? Are they unable to deal with simple problems without escalating the problem six levels in the organization? Or are they able to do what it takes to solve the customers' problems and do those extra little things that make a difference – and be recognized for doing so?

For a manager, the second application of C.E.O. Goals comes from looking at yourself as the Employee and looking at your employees as your Customer. Do your goals support your people and enhance their work environment? As has been shown in earlier chapters, the impact that supportive management has on reducing the costs of stress, such as

Chapter 7 – Building Systems That Work

absenteeism and prescription drug use, is massive. Supporting your people is not only the right thing to do ethically. It is also the right thing to do for the financial success of the company.

Relevance

In the basic system, this element was the *Gap* between the current state and your desired goal. For organizations, this gap must be relevant to the person who can bridge it.

While employee goals may be aligned with the customer and organizational goals, they may not be *relevant* to the employee. You may set customer satisfaction as a goal, but if the staff is punished or reprimanded for doing anything out of the ordinary, you won't get it. The threat of punishment not only damages the employee's personal power, it creates a goal of self-preservation that is far more important than your customer satisfaction goals.

Perhaps I am naive, but I believe we are all good people who want to do the best. Unfortunately, we are besieged by demands and expectations. We simply can't keep up with all of them and we have to focus on those that are most relevant: those that give us the most benefit or that could cause the most difficulty. The challenge is making sure the goals you want are the ones that are most relevant to your staff, at all levels.

A prime example of relevance is the traditional model of a salesperson on commission. An experienced salesperson knows that trust is incredibly hard to gain, and easy to lose, so you don't push things that the customer doesn't need. She knows that if you find a way to consistently add value to the customer, you'll make more over the lifetime of that customer. If you don't have the best solution now, tell them, and your sale will be easier next time. To this person, meeting the customer needs takes precedence.

In contrast, a hungry salesperson who has bills to pay, or a novice sales rep, isn't going to care about long-term sales. He needs money *now* and is going to push the sale, even if it loses him the customer. As a result, these people are always making the first sale – the hardest sale – and they are always struggling.

These two types of people have the same goal and commission system, but the relevant gap is different. For the experienced salesperson, meeting the customer satisfaction gap is most important because she knows that her long-term success will come with that. For the hungry sales rep, the only gap that's relevant is his lack of money now, and it drives completely different behaviour and produces completely different results.

Just like the hungry salesperson, many managers are driven by short-term results. They are held accountable for the budget or for performance *this quarter*. After decades of doing "less with more," there is little fat to spare. All resources have to be shunted into pushing performance, which drives crisis management, increases stress levels, and sabotages the long-term success of the organization. While the managers may know this intellectually, they are driven by the need to provide short-term results, and so create a downward spiral of struggle that gets harder and harder to recover from. As this struggle intensifies, the helplessness and stress levels of these managers increase. The system creates this feeling of helplessness and impairs the functioning of these people in doing their jobs.

Responsibility and Accountability

In aligning goals and making them relevant, responsibility and accountability have to go hand in hand. Far too often, staff are given only one without the other. This increases both their sense of helplessness and their stress levels, and hurts the organization.

Employees may be held accountable for delivering results that they can't control – that they don't have the authority or the responsibility to produce. Often employees are held accountable for upsetting a customer when they have no ability to address the customers' needs.

Alternatively, a staff member may have responsibility over an area, but not be held accountable for making the desired results happen. In many organizations I've seen initiatives launched and responsibilities allocated for making the changes happen. Then the individuals responsible for making the changes are not held accountable for the results. Too many other changes happen and the project slips on the agenda and then disappears. There is no clear win for making the change happen, or a clear penalty for not making it happen, and so it never comes to pass.

Giving individuals the ability and resources to take on a project, and obtaining their commitment to a time frame to make it happen are all elements of aligning their goals with the organization and the customer. Ensuring that there is a clear win for attaining that goal and holding them accountable for making it happen are aspects of making the gap relevant to them.

How Goal Alignment and Relevance Drive Results

A friend and mentor of mine used to be a problem-solver for UPS. In this unionized environment (he dealt with the Teamsters), he was able to turn around situations in a matter of days that had stalemated previous managers. He did this simply by respecting the people who worked for him, aligning their goals, and making them relevant.

A prime example is one facility that my friend was called in to deal with. The night shift, which unloaded the trailers and loaded the trucks, was disenchanted with the company and had gone on a work slowdown. The drivers worked from 8am until 5pm. If the trucks didn't get onto the road on time, anything after 5pm was overtime, and this happened daily. UPS put three managers in there, one a year, and they couldn't straighten out the problem. So UPS called in my friend.

He arrived on a Thursday night and the manager he was replacing introduced him to everybody. He stood around and observed that everybody was mad at everybody. The next night, Friday, he took some of the workers aside and asked them "what is the matter with you guys? I never have been able to understand anybody that would come to work and not be happy. I mean, being miserable at work is stupid."

In response, the workers called him all kinds of four-letter words, and said they'd been telling people for years and nobody had listened. My friend persisted, and they finally told him what was upsetting them. The root problem turned out to be the company's annual Christmas party, which had been held for the drivers for three years. Unfortunately, it had been on the days these employees worked, during their shift. The workers told him they'd like the party on a Saturday night, but none of the managers would come up from New York City on a Saturday for the party.

Another problem was that when the trucks were late, the night shift would have to clean the building, despite the fact that there was a full-time janitor to do that. My friend asked them what else they'd like to do during the time when they had nothing else to do. They said, "well, we like to play ping pong."

On Saturday, my friend bought two ping-pong tables out of his own pocket, snuck them into the loading docks and set them up. When the workers came in that Monday night, he said, "okay, here are the ping-pong tables, and the deal is this: No matter what happens, these vehicles have to be loaded on time." And they agreed.

That night, they had the trucks loaded and finished their shift 45 minutes before the end of the shift.

The biggest problem my friend had was moving the party. He did it, but it took a lot of work to get the management in New York to attend it at a time the workers from the loading dock could attend.

As is usually the case, what the workers wanted – the root cause of the problem – was minor. The problem was, none of the three previous managers had listened to them. They had been focused on the results, not on their people. My friend simply found out what the employees wanted, aligned their goals with his (the company's) goals, and made the gap relevant to the employees. What he could do, he did. When there's something he couldn't do, he told them he couldn't do it. The result: an immediate and lasting increase in productivity for the price of a couple of ping-pong tables and the time of a few managers.

Feedback
There are two broad categories for effective feedback. First is information on how you are doing so that you can fine-tune your course and stay on-track. Second is the recognition and reward systems that support the desired behaviour with commensurate wins.

Feedback can consist of verbal and written communication from superiors and peers. Reward and recognition systems can be financial, based on performance, or they can consist of a simple pat on the back or public recognition of good behaviour. All need to support the key goals addressed in the previous two elements of the system (alignment and relevance).

When providing feedback in the form of information, one of the greatest challenges is giving the appropriate amount of information. Too many people get too much information and can't weed out what's important, or they get no information and only get feedback in the form of penalties when they make a mistake.

No matter what job you have, you can distill the results down to 3-5 things that you need to keep on track. If you are to keep these things on track, then you need frequent, simple, timely feedback on those key things, and those alone. If you are setting C.E.O. Goals, then you need regular feedback on the C.E.O. Goals that you impact and are held accountable for.

Many people talk about the importance of customer satisfaction. If I'm talking to a roomful of people, and I ask how important it is, I'll get responses saying it's incredibly important, or the number one priority. "If it's so important," I ask then, "how many of you can tell me exactly what your customer satisfaction rating was yesterday? Or last week?" Rarely will anyone put up a hand.

If it's important, then it should be something that you know day-by-day, or at least week-by-week. Otherwise, there are the things that you *say* are important, like the values on the walls, and the things that really *are* important, like the values you see in the halls. Perhaps you're busy and have difficulty giving positive feedback because of the demands on you. If so, your actions show your real values. If your stated priorities are supposed to be so important, and your people are *not* getting simple, timely feedback on it, then what *is* the feedback they're receiving? Do they only get feedback when something goes wrong and they wind up in trouble?

If your people don't know how they're doing, then how can they do their job effectively? If they don't know how they're performing in their work, and are waiting for someone to blame them for a problem, what impact will that have on their personal power and on the company's productivity?

What if employees do something extra? Are they recognized in a positive way for it? If they go out of their way for a customer or a fellow employee, are they chastised, ignored, or rewarded? If an employee is chastised or ignored, that is a sure-fire way to kill that type of behaviour and destroy the personal power of all employees, not just that one. If individual employees are recognized and rewarded, then all employees will be more likely to do such things in the future. You generally get more of what you focus on.

By recognition, I don't mean always financial. Above a basic level, money simply doesn't motivate long-term – recognition does. The research is pretty solid on that. Simply recognizing them publicly, or having awards for specific desired behaviours makes a huge difference. People may feel a little embarrassed or bashful at being pointed out, but they love it. It enhances personal power and it produces measurable results, as long as the requirements for the recognition are clear, and the awards are given with discretion only to those who have earned them.

Whenever I work with an organization, I usually build in a whole range of simple awards that fit the culture and objectives. These awards may consist of simple recognition, or a series of pins as specific rewards for specific behaviours, or financial bonuses. The key is to focus on the behaviours the organization wants, and to reward them accordingly.

Unfortunately, problems are recognized (with criticism and/or penalties) far more often than excellent behaviour. The stick generally serves to decrease personal power and performance. The carrot works far better in building personal power and productivity. People can be forced to do 'satisfactory' work. If you want them to consistently push the envelope and go out of the way to move you ahead, they have to *want* to do so. And that means giving them clear wins that they value for doing so.

Yet another problem faced by many organizations is that feedback is purely financial. Managers need to know how they are doing as leaders, and how their people are doing. A manager's job is not to *do* anything – it's to make sure something *gets done*, and that something is done by their people. Thus, they have to know how effective they are as leaders. Factors such as leadership and staff personal power need to be measured on a regular basis. Managers have to be held accountable for such numbers, as they are what will drive long-term financial success and productivity.

There is a simple system, by the way, for measuring something even better than customer satisfaction on a daily basis. We have implemented it in restaurants, banks, stores, and even in the military. Customer satisfaction itself is actually obsolete. Researchers have found that our standards have gone up so much now that 'satisfactory' really isn't that great any more, and it doesn't impact repurchase. What makes the difference is how the customer *felt* about the service encounter. Customers who *loved* doing business with you are much more likely to repurchase.

What we do is give each customer a poker chip after the service encounter. At the door, there is a box with five vertical tubes and a slot at the top of each tube. At one end of the slots is a happy face, and at the other end is a frowning face. The customer is asked to drop their poker chip in the slot that best describes how she *felt* about her service encounter. This system provides simple, daily ratings on the one factor that determines repurchase. If customers drop their chip towards the frowning slot, then usually the staff will know why that happened. Employees are then given the responsibility for coming up with ideas on how to improve the results, and held accountable for doing so.

A variation of this can be used as a simple way to measure a team's level of personal power on a daily basis. Each employee can have a chip that they use on a scale that measures how much power, freedom and ability she feels to do her job that day. That is a measurement that both the manager and the team can use to improve the performance of the team on that scale on an ongoing basis.

Actions
Effective organizational systems have a clearly stated vision, values that are lived daily and consistently, align their goals and make the gap relevant, and provide simple, timely feedback to their people. These organizations then step out of the way and allow their people to take the action they require, freeing their actions and unleashing their personal

power. Ineffective organizations write policy manuals and create bureaucracies.

Policies tend to be formed when something goes wrong to ensure that it doesn't happen again. They punish the majority for the sins of the minority, and often cost the organization far more than the original problem. Extensive bureaucracy demotivates the workforce and drives down personal power.

A century ago, at the start of the industrial revolution, there was a need for bureaucracies to build the infrastructures that form the basis of modern society. Things didn't change that quickly, and the average worker had a grade four education. Today, the average worker has at least some post-secondary education. With competition, technology, and all the other changes we're dealing with, things are changing far too fast to develop policy that is meaningful any more. Ironically, the more policy manuals grow, the more holes appear, and rules and regulations constantly have to grow faster and faster to try to overcome the gaps, which grow even faster.

Beyond the costs of the process and the costs of stress, bureaucratic systems have an added cost to the organization. Controlling and constraining your people gives a clear message that they aren't trusted or respected, and there is often a backlash for this. People in one organization couldn't access the tools they needed for work without signatures, so they rationalized getting back at the company by taking pens and other office supplies home.

The owner of a bar took $8 off each of his wait staff's paychecks to pay for the pop and coffee that they drank. In response, the wait staff would stand around and chat after closing, holding the pop dispenser open over the sink for an hour at a time, or constantly replacing each others' drinks after they had taken only one sip. There's always payback, and employees who feel they've been wronged generally know exactly how to hurt the organization in kind.

In many retail stores, before staff can leave, their managers have to search their bags and other personal belongings to be sure the employees aren't stealing anything. The impact of such demeaning practices on personal power is obvious. The goals of the staff are not aligned and the most relevant goal will likely be to 'get back' at the store in some way.

What the employees do in such all-too-common situations may not be right, but if they are treated without respect or trust, they will treat their employer the same way. And this treatment certainly doesn't build loyalty, commitment, or the desire to go out of their way for the organization. Ironically, these employees' behaviours often result in new restrictive policies and procedures, which lead to further reactive behaviours – a vicious, self-perpetuating system of distrust that drains the productivity of organizations.

How Cultural Systems Create Results

Recently I was called in to work with a call center that was about to lose a major contract selling credit cards for a bank. This call center had to double sales within two weeks to keep the contract, and we did so by simply applying the systems framework described here.

Traditionally, this facility had been an inbound call center, where customers called in for information or to purchase items. The contract they were having difficulty with was their first outbound sales contract, where their people had to call customers to make sales. Outbound sales is a whole different world than inbound sales.

This company had assigned some of their regular staff and supervisors to the job without any supplemental training. These people did a great job in the inbound environment, where the biggest challenges were responding quickly and completing the call to time and quality specifications. They didn't know what to do in the new environment.

The people on the phone felt uncomfortable making the calls, and they were ill-equipped to do so. With little support, no training, and income based on commission for the first time, the pressure was on. Nobody knew how they did until the end of the night, unless they happened to keep score themselves. Usually employees didn't do that because sales were so low they were demotivating. If somebody next to them made a sale, it demotivated them even further. These people were incredibly stressed and unhappy.

The supervisors didn't know how to manage the performance when it fell short because they had no experience in coaching, and they didn't really know how to do that job themselves. Thus, when things got tough, they reverted to classical authoritarian stereotypes. The supervisors were abrupt and got upset at people when they didn't perform. They weren't happy either and were also very stressed.

Over the first couple of weeks of the contract they tried many things, but little of what they had done had been effective because of their lack of experience. Teams were set up, but nobody knew who was on their team, and the members were scattered around the center. They had a budget for incentives, but didn't know how to use them. For example, they bought lottery tickets and walked around handing them to everyone instead of to people who made sales. They rewarded people for sitting at their seats, rather than for performing well.

One of the first things that I did was to reassign two of the three supervisors. They simply did not have the skill set for the job, or the desire to develop it, and they didn't really want to be there anyway. They were supervisors because they had been there longer than anyone else and so were promoted. This is absolutely the worst reason for putting someone in a job, particularly if they don't have the skill set or inclination for it. One of these people was moved into a technical support position and the other back into a supervisory position in the inbound division. Both loved and appreciated these changes.

I eliminated the job 'supervisor' and created a new one: 'coach.' The third supervisor was able to adapt to the new position. Two people off the phones who had the skill set and interest to be coaches were also selected for this new role. The compensation for these three coaches was a fixed salary and a bonus. The bonus was based on the performance of the entire group to make the performance gap relevant and give the coaches a stake in the success of the whole group. An accelerated and on-the-job training and coaching program was provided for both them and the call center manager to help them in their jobs.

The people on the phones were put into teams. The teams were positioned together in pods, so they all sat together. I pulled each team off the phones for a few hours at a time, which the call center had been afraid to do because of fears of lost productivity. In this time, I

Chapter 7 – Building Systems That Work

provided the employees with some basic rapport building and selling skills so that they felt they had some support. This feeling of being supported was probably more important than the actual skills that they were taught.

All teams included some high performers and low performers to enable coaching within each team. The compensation was changed to a mixture of individual and team bonus, so that whenever someone in the pod make a sale, it meant that everyone on the team won. Hearing others do well motivated them instead of disillusioning them: simple goal alignment and gap relevance.

Because of the short time frame, we went low-tech with a huge whiteboard hung on the most visible wall as our main channel for feedback. On this board, key statistics for the whole group and for each team were updated hourly (sales for the night, average sales per hour for the night, sales for the last hour and average sales per hour for the last hour). Each team also had a whiteboard in each pod to track their individual and team performance.

The incentive budget was channeled into all sorts of incentives that aligned the goals to keep up the energy hour by hour. You can produce a lot more with a turned on team having fun than you can with one working under fear and pressure. We made sure we recognized things such as best improved as well as best sales for the night or for an hour, so that there were goals that were relevant to everyone.

If an individual was having difficulty, one of the coaches would work with them and focus them on specific tasks with specific improvement goals to enhance their performance. If a team was having difficulty, we might pull them off the phones for a quick meeting to have them revitalize themselves and solve their problem. Sometimes the coaches or I would get on the phones to challenge them. We did whatever it took to support them and to make it fun, and the results happened.

At call centers, supervisors traditionally listen in to a couple of calls a week for each person on the phone. A supervisor scores the employee on a quality sheet, checking specific things the staff member needs to do each call. She then reviews these scores with the staff member to improve their performance. It worked fine in the inbound environment, but here, with the added pressure of selling, quality ratings had dropped to sixty percent or so. The employees could only deal with so much, and the quality feedback had little impact. When I changed their compensation system to include team-based bonuses, the commission was increased slightly and multiplied by their average quality rating for the week. All of a sudden the quality score feedback was relevant and they started scoring 95-100%.

All of these results come from the systems approach outlined in this chapter. The goals were aligned, the gap made relevant, and simple, timely feedback systems were set up. They more than doubled sales in two weeks. We increased the personal power of the people on the front line (and those supervising them), supported them, and they took all the actions required. They won. The call center won. And they had a whole lot of fun in the process.

'Systems' Mean More Than Just Financial Rewards

While financial incentives are part of cultural systems, they are a small part of the systems that drive an organization. Perhaps the best example I can give of modifying behaviour using non-financial systems is my experience teaching in universities over the past several years.

University students have no financial incentive to perform better. The only apparent incentive is their marks, but marks are only relevant because most instructors don't invest the time to align the *real* goals of the students and make learning relevant.

When I started teaching, I went in knowing that the traditional methods of lecturing and testing had little to do with long-term learning, and certainly with understanding the reality of something like business. You can't learn it from a textbook. My goal was to have the students learn how to think and, hopefully, learn something that would be useful to them in their careers. To do this, I had to align their personal goals with my goal, and make my goal relevant to them.

The first thing I did was find out what was important to each of them. Then I put them in groups where they complemented and built on each others' backgrounds and interests. Like most instructors, I received 100-150 new students each term. I wanted to build their sense of personal power by knowing each of them individually. I used little tricks like taking pictures of each group and posting them above my desk, and I could call them all by name within a week or two. In this way, they weren't just a number, and I found out more about them. They knew I cared about them. By investing that time, I was able to make a connection with most of them and make the goals relevant by linking the core skills I was teaching to their individual career aspirations.

Often, we agreed to the grade up front to get it out of the way, and I told them what they needed to do to get it. I treated them as if they were my employees, and they acted as consultants doing real work for real businesses – they made a difference. Each student received detailed, targeted feedback from me to build the specific skills and knowledge base I was targeting.

The result? They invested hours upon hours into their 'consulting' projects – more than in any other course usually – and produced amazing results for their 'clients.' I can run into former students today, a decade later, and they still remember their project and what they did – and they can't even remember what other courses they took. They attended virtually every class, and were actively involved. They developed the critical thinking skills that they needed in their careers. And, along the way, they learned the subject material for the courses they took, and earned great grades.

No financial incentives. And yet I gained the commitment and involvement of the students and they accomplished the learning that I wanted. I taught them very little. They taught themselves, all because of systems, and they loved it.

Putting Systems Into Practice

Am I suggesting that you throw out your policy manuals and destroy bureaucracy overnight? Certainly not – that would be instant disaster. However, policy manuals and bureaucracies are enemies of personal power, and they likely limit the productivity and effectiveness of your organization far more than they help. If you really want to enhance the personal power and the productivity of your people, then you need to look at the cultural systems to find out how you're holding them back. You also need to put hard numbers on concepts such as personal power and leadership, and you have to start from the top of the organization down. All of this takes a great deal of concerted effort, depending on how much bureaucracy you have to start with. So be fully committed, and commit the resources you need before you begin.

Chapter 8 – Leading the Way

Cultural systems are learned ways of doing things based on experience. The greatest influence on these systems is management, particularly senior management. If you want to change your cultural systems to enhance personal power and productivity, it has to start with your leaders.

Effective leadership has been talked about for decades. The same principles that have been presented in many leadership texts are the principles that enhance personal power and reduce stress – the essence of supportive management. In this chapter, the approaches of five effective leaders from different industries, from large organizations and small, are explored. While they have different personalities, the core principles that they employ are consistent. All of them build cultural systems that grow personal power and tap their people to produce results far beyond most organizations. The words of the leader profiled are italicized in each section below.

Manufacturing – Matt Guerin

Larson-Juhl is the leading firm in the picture-molding and accessories market. When you order a picture frame at a frame shop, that order will often go to Larson-Juhl to fulfill. Larson-Juhl runs its company by six core values:

- Customer always comes first
- Fairness and honesty in all dealings
- Respect for the individual
- Excellence in products and service
- Rewards tie to performance
- Leadership by example

They reinforce and support these values in a variety of ways. Most notable is the Gold Values Award, given to the facility that best lives these values. Evaluation for this award is rigorous and comprehensive. You have to have it all – living the values, teamwork, quality, sales and profitability.

105

Matt Guerin is a multiple winner of the Gold Values Award for the
facilities that he has run. He started with Larson Juhl in sales in 1989.
A year later, he opened their first manufacturing facility in Phoenix.
After two years there, he moved to Cincinnati to start a facility there,
and then was sent to Detroit (where he is originally from) to turn
around a facility that was not working well. Matt is now a Regional
Manager, looking after several of these plants. He creates systems that
support his people and build productivity.

For Matt, there are two building blocks that are always in place. The
first is made up of the mission and the values. When his people made a
decision, all they need to stay on track is to check themselves against
the mission and the values. Next are the goals for the desired results.
His people know what the goals are for sales and expenses. Their
personal wins are aligned with those, and that system keeps them on
track.

What do Values Mean?
As with any business, a core challenge was translating the values into
what was expected for day-to-day behaviour. Matt invested the time to
ensure that his people understood what actions the values called for,
and also what they didn't mean. Investing that time brought both
Cincinnati and Detroit the results – and Gold Values Awards from
Larson-Juhl.

*I explained to them scenarios within Larson-Juhl and outside Larson-
Juhl, what I saw as excellent products and services. I painted a pretty
specific picture with examples, and I think that was crucial. We
showed what it would not look like as well. We even compared other
facilities in other organizations that were clearly not doing the right
things or achieving the results and really broke down why that was
happening.*

*Over 3 years, Cincinnati won two Gold Values Awards and one Silver
Award. The team in Detroit actually went down to Cincinnati and saw
it first-hand. They saw what the facility looked like, how the team
members interacted. When they went down, they were a little skeptical.
But when they came back, they communicated everything.*

Chapter 8 – Leading the Way

Goal Alignment

To Matt, the most critical step in goal alignment is ensuring that you have the right people on-board. Cincinnati was a startup, and Matt was able to ensure that the people he brought on had the same commitment and vision he did. In Detroit, it called for changing many of the people who were there. He actually hired back some people who had been let go, and he turned those who had been named 'problem employees' into champions.

When I got there, I was told there were some team members that had poor performance, poor attitudes, and others that were obviously very strong. And I found in most cases, the reverse of that. The team members that I was told had attitudes were the best ones. They just wanted change. They had ideas, and they wanted improvements, and they were unable to unleash a lot of those talents.

Detroit had high turnover before Matt arrived, and he created 60-70% turnover in his first year to ensure that he had the right people. The following year, when they won the Gold Values Award, turnover was less than 10%.

In order to determine whether or not his people were on-board, Matt was absolutely clear about his goals and expectations.

We made it very clear what the goals and expectations were, and I shared with them what my vision was. Then I hit some one-on-one conversations, and just asked, "are you on board?" Some were, some were not.

We built a culture that was focused on serving the customer. We worked very hard. However, we made sure we were having fun in the process. Once I made clear what everyone's roles and everyone's goals were, we were able to do that.

Once the team was in place, Matt turned his focus to creating the right environment – a clean, organized, fun facility. They painted the entire facility, and then worked together to clean up each area as a team. He created a sense of ownership and showed them very visible results that they themselves created.

Within a matter of a month, we had that place, probably one of the worst looking facilities in terms of cleanliness and organization, to one of the best. I'm a firm believer that if you have high expectations of team members, you've got to put them in an environment to be successful.

Next, he asked his people if they had the right equipment, and they gave him a long shopping list. Despite some questions from head office, he bought them the equipment they needed to do the job right, and they saw that he was serious.

After that, the next step we did (and this is we, not I) is we set what the goals were, and after that started achieving them. I say 'we,' because they've got to be totally involved in the process. No involvement, no commitment, and they're really committed to their goals.

As opposed to setting goals for people and demanding that they achieve them, Matt engaged his people in establishing the goals, so that they owned them. This built their sense of personal power, and thus their commitment and productivity.

Relevance

One of Larson-Juhl's values is 'reward outstanding performance.' Matt talked with his people about what those rewards looked like to make them relevant. Monetarily, he shared what their raises could look like if they achieved at a very high level. He also shared with them what the profit-sharing would look like, as well as the size of the payment they could expect from winning the Gold Values Award.

I paid people based on the performance, and we paid people very well. I'd much rather have less people, but higher qualified and higher producers, to reap those benefits. And by doing that, you have fewer errors which lead to expenses. You have less inventory, which improves bottom line.

Matt also personalized the rewards for each employee. If the team hit its goal, and there was a financial reward, say of $40, this figure was translated into something specific that each employee liked. They could simply buy what they wanted for $40 and turn in an expense form.

Chapter 8 – Leading the Way

We had one team member who was into golf. He could turn in a round of golf, and that would take care of that expense form, or he could wait a whole year, saving for a set of golf clubs. We had some that were readers. I know one person was saving the money for her child's Christmas, which I thought was beautiful. The thing that was nice was that goal was in front of her all year – what the reward looked like.

'Rewards' means a lot of different things to a lot of different people. In a lot of cases, it's the recognition. A pat on the back that you did a good job. We celebrated a lot, and we recognized a lot as well.

Now that the employees knew the goals and the gap was made relevant, they acted to resolve the issues, as opposed to handing them up to management as in the past.

It put the responsibility back on the saw operators to be creative and find what the issue was and then work out the solution themselves. They knew that they could take whatever steps were necessary to resolve an issue and take care of a customer. And it took a while for them to really understand that they had the authority always to make that decision.

Freeing Actions

Larson-Juhl as a company does keep its eye on the bottom line. However, they free each General Manager to produce the results they want, and hold them accountable for those results. They don't question every expense and tie the hands of their people. As Matt was free, so did he free his people to deliver the results he wanted.

For us, it was simply the proof. We did some pretty wild things in terms of a lot of lunches and a lot of purchases of shirts and things like that, and it led to more profitability. Clearly, every year, when you saw the sales growth, the expense reduction, and also the income, there was no question.

Feedback

It took a little time and some effort for Matt to develop the personal power of his people and their confidence in making the decisions, even if in some cases they may not have been the best decisions. He was looking at the long-term development of his people and of his team.

You just need to support every one of their decisions. In the back of my mind, there were a couple that I said something to myself – not to them. I bit my tongue and never questioned any of their decisions. I'd say "it's your decision. And just remember that you've got to live with the impact and implications of this." And it's like, "Wow! It truly is mine."

Matt gave his team all the information about the business so that they could make the best decisions for the company, overall. They knew how they were performing on their goals, and they knew how those goals impacted them, personally.

We over-communicated the impact on the financials. So they clearly knew the cost of a product, the expense involved in an error. The more they knew about the business and the impact of errors, the better their decisions.

We took an example. One of the products we sell is a mat board, and this mat board at our cost, is $2.07. Maybe we sell it for $3.10. We said, "what if this customer got this mat board and it was the wrong one? Let's walk through all the steps that happen to replace this." Again the cost. We created the scenario that it was a customer in Northern Michigan and they had to have it on Saturday. By the time everything was done and said, we figured the cost to our company was probably $278 to replace that two dollar mat board, in terms of the people involved, the system time, UPS. That doesn't even calculate the frustration on the part of the customer and the impact it had on his customer. So that really opened up some eyes and they developed the solution.

Taking It Up a Level

Now as a Regional Manager looking after several such manufacturing facilities, Matt applies the same principles to produce broader-based results. Matt very much considers himself a 'servant leader,' helping his people succeed.

Chapter 8 – Leading the Way

There are some parallels. They still have the autonomy to make the decisions. I need to give them as much information from the corporate end, which they weren't exposed to in the past, in terms of what our goals were, cash flow, margins, future positioning, strategic planning, things along those lines. We're working together on what the goals are. And they see that, more than anything, I have their best interests at heart. You can talk about values, but when they see it in what you do, that makes an impact.

Health Care – Anne McGuire

In the 1990's, Nova Scotia was implementing health care reform, which basically meant rationalization and cuts. Most hospital CEOs did nothing in this uncertain environment, waiting for some clear sense of direction. When that direction came, their jobs were eliminated, replaced by regional CEOs.

Instead of waiting and doing nothing, Anne McGuire, the new CEO of the Nova Scotia Hospital, the primary mental health care facility in the province, led a groundbreaking strategic planning initiative that managed the cuts and effectively reinvented mental health care in a way that had never been done before.

We got involved in huge changes through a very difficult period when a lot of people just sort of stopped and waited for something to happen to them.

In doing this, she engaged the customers (the consumers of mental health services) and the employees in the entire process, giving them a sense of control, commitment and buy-in that ultimately created their success. She developed program-based mental health care, where different health professionals worked together as a cohesive team.

People are inherently wanting to do good things, the right things, and everyone makes a contribution in some way, shape or form. If you can just find a way to free people up to use what they've got, they want to do the right thing, they want to do positive things. And they can't do that in an atmosphere of mistrust.

The strategic planning initiative was anchored in measuring key factors. It started with focus groups of consumers to find out what the

111

hospital was doing right and what wasn't working to point out what needed to change.

Baseline and follow up staff satisfaction surveys were taken to measure the impact of the initiatives that were launched. In addition, the staff was asked to vote periodically on what they thought were the most important accomplishments to date, or on what were the most critical areas to address. These more 'formalized' processes complemented ongoing feedback.

Vision

Behind the entire initiative was Anne's vision.

I've never been able to understand how people who had brain diseases, psychiatric disorders are so marginalized and stigmatized in our society. Part of my drive, and I think this is true for the people I work with too, is a really genuine wish to make a real difference for that group of people. And I think that we are.

While it was likely that the changes in the health care system would eventually absorb this hospital (which it eventually did), Anne was committed to making the Nova Scotia Hospital the best it could be, a model of how organizational change could work effectively. This task was even more of a challenge when psychiatric hospitals were generally seen as 'lesser beings' in the broader health care system.

Values

Like her vision, the values that Anne operated by were clear and well defined: Open communication, involvement, empowerment, and a healthy workplace.

However unlike many organizations that develop values statements, Anne and her team actually used these values as guides for decision making and for their day-to-day behaviours. They went beyond rhetoric. When they were in a difficult position, they asked each other "what is the right thing to do – morally, ethically, and for the greatest good of the people we serve?"

We are a mental health facility so we should know about trying to reduce stress.

112

The linkage is clear in the actions, systems and overall strategy. Communication was the prime key to their success. Anne involved her staff at all levels and she also involved her customers (the consumers of mental health services) on the committees, on the Board, and even on clinical teams. She passed the power on through initiatives such as the business planning process. Measures, such as the staff satisfaction survey, showed their progress in building a healthy workplace.

Finally, of course, her personal values – honesty, integrity, openness, sharing, and a respect for everyone's contribution – were fully aligned with the organizational values that guided her work.

Communication

The one thread that runs through all of Anne's work is communication. This focus was critical to understanding, aligning, and communicating goals, and to providing effective feedback on progress. It's virtually impossible to over-communicate, and most implementations fall short because of under-communication. Information was passed on using e-mail, bulletin boards, redesigned newsletters and brochures. The executive understood very clearly that the time when they were tired of saying something was the time that their people were just starting to really hear it.

Every decision we made as an executive group had to have a corresponding communication piece attached to it. We would try to keep the organization 100% informed on everything that we were doing, thinking, trying out.

When information had to be passed on to the staff, members of the executive group would meet with the management group and brief them on the issues. They would then issue scripts to the management group so that every one of the people in the organization would get exactly the same words, without any distortion.

Rumors

Two of the certainties in any organization are that rumors will fill any lack of information, and that rumors propagate and travel faster than any other information. Anne's team dealt with rumors head-on.

People would, in some circumstances, rather believe the rumors than the actual truth because they're generally more exciting, though frightening.

Their most important strategy was to be visible and to know people well enough so they could ask any questions they had, and so that they could share rumors with management. Without knowing what the rumors are, it's hard to counter them. Anne's team had fun with this, having open forums asking what the latest rumors were and addressing them.

Walkabouts

Twice a year, Anne's team took all of their strategic results and presented them to the entire staff. They put up posters representing these results all over the walls of the auditorium, and the champions for each initiative presented their results. This event was made into a great celebration with balloons and food and prizes over a day. Staff came in when they were able and wandered around, finding out about the specific projects, and about the greater context into which each piece fit.

If you can't see the whole of where you're going – the vision – and you can't understand the external and internal context of where it is you're trying to go, then it's very hard to motivate people or to have them understand what their piece of it is.

Access to Information

Before Anne's time, the CEO's office had special locks and only handpicked cleaning people were allowed to clean it. Such systems drain personal power and increase depersonalization and stress because of the lack of trust and respect they create. That has all changed. Personnel-related and legal documents are locked up, or stored elsewhere, but everything else is open.

My philosophy is, if somebody wants to come and read my files, then maybe they'll learn something. There really are no secrets here. There's nothing except personal information about employees that people can't know about in terms of everything that's going on in healthcare.

Chapter 8 – Leading the Way

It's always been amazing to me that people in management and senior management positions seem to have an attitude that information is power, and that if you give it away, you give away your power. If you have a choice between keeping something and giving it away, I can't understand why you wouldn't choose to give it away as long as you're confident that you're giving it to the right people for the right reasons.

We should constantly be giving away our power to the point where you almost have none. As you keep giving away the power, you make your organization stronger. That's why we're here. To make a strong organization, to make better programs for patients, and to have people all through the organization feel that they have a piece of that.

It is this type of philosophy in action that builds the personal power of people. Hoarding information from your people (even if that information is that you don't know what's going on) only builds their helplessness and stress levels. And the fact is that, if you don't know the answer to their questions, they know, even if you don't tell them you don't know.

Letting Go

Before she took over as CEO, Anne saw her organization flounder under a succession of leaders who kept a tight hold on information and power. Some would state values such as freedom of expression, with no penalty for doing so. Then, when someone did express their opinion, there were all kinds of recriminations.

Most people in hospitals don't have the opportunity to use the school of knowledge that they have and people are constantly frustrated by the restrictions that they feel by management, processes, and decisions. I think that's a tremendous waste of a resource. It's a tremendous disincentive to bright people who don't hang around if that's the environment they perceive they're working in. It's important that people can use the knowledge that they've got, in the context of the larger, big picture, and if they don't know about that, I just don't understand how they can really do an effective piece of work.

We're here to look after patients, so the most important people here are the people who are doing that, and if they don't know what tools they've got and what the realities are and where they fit in, it just doesn't seem to me that they can work and feel satisfied.

Instead of a top-down business planning process, Anne's team sent planning down to the frontline. The entire plan is put together with grassroots involvement. While it takes longer, the ownership and commitment is built in, as is the increased personal power of the people throughout the organization. They feel they have some sense of control of what's happening to them.

To further build personal power, the plan is available to everybody, including the union. In fact, after reviewing the plan, the union filed a couple of policy grievances, which Anne listened to.

Being Accessible

People are starting to talk about the soul of organizations and I believe that that's a really important part of how organizations function. I tend to pay more attention to the emotions of the organization as opposed to the structures.

Investing the time in relationships is of paramount importance to Anne, whether those are relationships with her staff, her customers, or external organizations. It is this time that builds the personal power of her people and helps her understand what their goals are so she can keep them aligned and relevant.

There are six hundred people who work here and I think I know most of them by their first name. I try to find out who they are. If there are major issues, I'm aware of them. The key thing is being available, being visible, being open, understanding what other people need and how they can get it from me. You have to be in touch.

Professional Services – Kevin Hamm

Kevin Hamm is the C.E.O. of Pharmasave Atlantic, a cooperative of independent pharmacies. Pharmasave supplies its members with turnkey total operations including a flyer, advertising, in-store décor, and house brand products. When he took over in 1994, Pharmasave had just over $100 Million in sales, 43 stores, poor relationships with their suppliers, high turnover, high absenteeism, and was $500,000 in the red. This meant that the pharmacy owners who were members of the cooperative had to pay their franchise fees *plus* cover these losses.

Today, Pharmasave Atlantic has 80 member stores, $225 Million in sales, great supplier relations, and for every dollar the members pay in for franchise fees, they get all the services plus $1.60 back. Kevin runs a turned-on team at the head office that absolutely loves coming to work and produces results that escalate each year.

Turnover. We have the exact opposite. We have people knocking on the door trying to get in here.

1994 – The Year of the Fix

Before taking over Pharmasave Atlantic, Kevin was one of their suppliers. He worked for one of their wholesale distributors. He knew that their trading partners didn't trust them, because he was one of them, and he didn't trust the management team or the structure of the company.

When he walked into this position in May of 1994, there was a lack of trust and confidence within the team. Several people didn't talk to each other. They took no responsibility for themselves, and were playing each other off, and "dropping each other in the soup" (Kevin's term for blaming things on others when problems arose). It was very much a 'we/they' atmosphere, and not 'us' as a team.

We had people that weren't talking to each other. We had high, high turnover here. It was a revolving door. We had public displays of rage. When I first got here, a couple of the gals would talk to me about the 'Monday-Friday Syndrome.' I said "what's the 'Monday-Friday Syndrome?'" Well, Monday they don't come in because they had too much fun on the weekend. They don't want to come in here because they're not pumped up. And then Friday afternoon, they want to get out of here early and take off.

For Kevin, each year has a theme, and 1994 was the year of the fix. They had to fix the income statement and balance sheet and they did. In six months, the company was in the black, and these results *all* came from relationships. It all started from Kevin's very first day.

I asked for an 8 o'clock staff meeting my very first morning. Instead of walking around and introducing myself I came in here and I told them my belief system, and I told them about how I believed in hard work, honesty, and sincerity. And I believe that attitude, if it was married with honest, sincere, 100% effort would take us to whatever the 'Promised Land' was going to be. We'd have to figure out the 'Promised Land,' but that would take us there. Any compromise on it, and we wouldn't have any chance.

I know people are going to think that stuff is corny, but when you deliver it, day after day, week after week, month after month, it suddenly becomes buried in the culture. Then it's not corny. It's called culture. And people buy into it. They know you're not going to drop them in the soup.

Secondly, what I said is "I'm going prove this to you. Over the course of the next days, weeks, months, you may roll your eyes, you may even doubt me. You're going to see that I will deliver, and when I don't deliver, call me on it. Matter of fact, call anyone in this office on it. Once we sign off on what the qualities of a first-run office will be, you'll get a chance to call someone."

In order to define what the qualities of a 'first-run office' were, Kevin pulled his team together and asked everyone to talk about the best companies they ever worked for, and the traits of those companies. He put those on a flip chart. Kevin then asked, "what would be 'utopia?'" What would be the ultimate for this company here? The staff named five principles:

- being a productive individual
- being a trusted teammate
- delivering a fun and pleasant working environment
- taking risks/free thinking
- being a positive communicator

Kevin then took the next step and asked "what does it mean to be a trusted teammate?" and broke down each of the values into daily deliverables. At the end of it, he asked everyone if they would be willing to take a sign-off sheet and say "I will be a trusted teammate, I will be a positive communicator, as defined by these definitions."

118

Chapter 8 – Leading the Way

Not everyone could adapt to this open & candid culture. We actually had someone leave over it. Everyone else bought into it and signed off on these values.

It brought our team very close together. Everyone understood that, to have a very strong company, it started on the ground floor with strong individuals. It led then to strong teammates. It then led to a strong team. It starts with individuals. We just knew, before we could develop the store members, and the program, we had to be fundamentally sound as a team.

They wrote out the five elements of their values system and put it on a wall for the first couple of years. Then, Kevin pulled his team together and asked if they needed them up there, and they agreed they didn't. Their values were seen in the halls and didn't need to be on the walls. They now carry them on a wallet card with their mission on the other side.

Building the Systems to Support the Values

Many companies go through similar exercises to set up the values they would like to live by. That alone does nothing. These values and their associated behaviours have to be translated into aligned, relevant goals. You have to build systems that support and encourage them, and that is exactly what Kevin did.

For the first two years, they had an annual award for the team members who have best lived each of the five values. The top 3 names under each value were named at a special event. Reasons for nominations were listed before each name was mentioned. It was incredibly emotional for them, like winning an Academy Award, Kevin would say. This feedback system made the goals relevant to each team member. What's most important is that the staff nominated and voted for the winners, not Kevin.

We no longer have the annual awards for the five values. As a group we decided they were ingrained in us and did not need an award to deliver the five so we discontinued them after a two-year run.

Every second Friday, for the last eight years, everyone who's in the office gets together for an 'around the horn' meeting for a couple of hours. This meeting is not giving an update and it's not about numbers. Those are addressed in project meetings. This meeting is about expressing how each person feels.

Communication is togetherness. You have to stay together to do that. So we go 'around the horn' every second Friday, and we still do it now, eight years later. And we say, "Kevin, how are you feeling? What's going on?" The first couple of meetings a few of the shyer people didn't say anything. That's fine. After 3 or 4 meetings, they felt uncomfortable not saying anything, and they opened up. The system just puts them into a position of feeling so much comfort that they open up. They feel that they're with trusted teammates.

You can't force such trust. There has to be a genuine atmosphere of support and caring, modeled by the leader to allow this to work. That's why these meetings also include feeling upset with each other, including Kevin. Everyone is able to call their teammates on it if they didn't live up to the values they each signed off on.

We've had a few where someone has said "I don't feel like you people have supported me. I feel like someone may have dropped me in the soup." And we either get it out at this 'around the horn' meeting, or I'll do a side meeting to get it out. This vehicle lets them express that, and that's very, very healthy.

These meetings provide a safe environment to surface and deal with those things that create discomfort and tension in the work place, thus enhancing his team members' personal power and sense of control.

At Pharmasave Atlantic they run peer evaluations, including 'Hamm Evaluations.' Each year they appoint a different person to solicit comments on him from all the team members, and that person comes back and feeds it back to Kevin. He's not allowed contesting or challenging anything that is brought up at this meeting.

If ten people are telling me I act a certain way, I should realize I act a certain way. I come back to one of our 'around the horn' meetings, and I always thank them for their candid and honest expression, and I

120

give them a summary of it. "This is what you told me to keep doing. I realize I have to keep doing these things and I'm going to keep doing them. In terms of start doing, I realize I have to start putting these things in place, and I'm going to do it. In terms of stop doing, I didn't even realize this behaviour resided in me, so thank you very much for bringing it to my attention."

Sometimes I said "look folks, I want you to know that I hear you loud and clear that you want me to stop doing it. You have to understand, this is part of my job in how I report to the Board." After we had one of these sessions, someone came up to me and said "I didn't realize that the Board wanted you to report on this every month. Now I understand, and I will never put it down in the 'stop doing' again."

I should have explained it to them in the beginning, that "folks, one of the reasons I ask for this is that I have to give it to the Board."

Building Relevance and Ownership

Kevin helps his people understand that they can run their own business unit at Pharmasave. Without taking the risks of running their own businesses, without putting all their money on the line, his people can each run their own unit right there. Then Kevin finds ways to showcase those units while he takes a back seat.

Prior to me getting here, the Board meeting once a month was whoever was in my chair meeting with the Board of Directors. I talked the Board into having the departmental unit managers come in every month and give a report. They, for the first time ever, are reporting to a Board of Directors. They have to go in and deliver the goods. Most folks manage children, a family, a mortgage, a car payment, and everything else. If you gave them the autonomy to allow them to use their skills, and marry it with attitude, why wouldn't they take the responsibility?

In addition to being a specialist in their area of expertise, he expects every one of his people to also be a good generalist and to understand how and why the rest of the business functions. Every second Friday, one of his team members does a presentation to educate the rest of the staff on their area of expertise.

Then there's pride, and what comes with that pride is an understanding, and all of a sudden, empathy from the other teammates that say "I didn't know she did that. I didn't know he did that."

As a result of these meetings, each individual's goals are made more relevant as their ownership of their department grows. The staff also understands how their work fits in the broader context and what else affects their work. Such understanding again enhances personal power.

How to Deal With Failure

Kevin trumpets his team members' successes throughout the organization and beyond. Every success is a reason to celebrate and a great element of feedback. Failure is a different thing altogether.

I don't believe in public failure. I don't believe in public hanging. When people come into this company, we talk to them about 'learn, grow, win.' And if you have good intentions, do your homework, and have read the industry, you will learn, grow, and win. You will make mistakes. But you'll find that you're producing many more wins than losses.

Despite the fact that he deals with failures privately, the close-knit nature of the group means that everyone does find out. Kevin simply doesn't make it a spectacle, and he uses failures to help his people learn, grown and win.

One day one of his people told him another team member was upset because she made a mistake, so Kevin went to talk to her. It was a simple human error that cost the company money.

I said, "may I ask you some questions? You know what they're going to be. 1) Did you do your homework?" She said, "yeah." I said "2) Did you have good intentions? Did you really think you were doing the right thing?" She said, "yeah." Then I asked her, "3) Did you think that this initiative that you're doing fit into the big scheme of things – what we're trying to accomplish here at Pharmasave?" And she said, "yeah."

122

Chapter 8 – Leading the Way

*Then I jotted down her 9 previous initiatives, plus this one. On the first
9, I went 'home run, home run, home run, home run....' On the last
one I put 'Struck out,' and we both laughed, and I said to her, "if you
had nine strike-outs, we would have something serious to talk about,
especially if you didn't learn anything from it. Tell me what you
learned from this one here where you struck out," and she told me she
went too fast.*

*The bottom line is, I said "do you think it will ever happen again?"
She said "It never will happen again." I said, "then this has been a
great experience." Even when you make a mistake, if you learn and
grow and win from the mistake, then it's not a strikeout.*

Several things stand out here that show how Kevin lives the philosophy
he preaches. First, he went straight to talk to his team member as soon
as he heard that she was upset. Second, Kevin knew enough about
what she did that he could name her last 10 projects off the top of his
head. Third, he focused her back on his mantra of 'learn, grow and
win.' All of these behaviours reflect supportive management, which
enhances personal power, commitment and productivity.

Letting the Team Align Their Goals

Kevin tracked down a list of 10 things great companies did for their
employees, and took this list to his team. He asked them to pick out
what would make a difference to them, and the simplicity of what they
wanted shocked him – like a stocked fridge.

*We come in here, getting our kids off, doing this and doing that in the
morning. Sometimes we don't even get a bagel or a slice of bread or a
piece of fruit in the morning. They don't expect filet mignons in there.
They know we can't do that. But the mileage that we've got out of
having some fresh bagels and muffins and fresh fruit in the morning is
scary.*

When Kevin started at Pharmasave Atlantic, hardly any of his people
arrived at the office by 8:30, when office hours began. He had to insist
that they were in the office from 8:30 until 4:30.

*Since we did this, fresh fruit and bagels in the fridge, we have people in
here by 10 after 8. Quite a statement, isn't it?*

This initiative is a simple matter of goal alignment. Kevin didn't just implement the list he found, or throw it out because it was impractical. He gave his people the list and they told him what was important to them. He provided that, and the payback is many times his investment by simply giving the power back to his people.

How to Help Your Employees Find Better Jobs Elsewhere

One of Kevin's team members was offered a job – the job of his dreams, in fact – elsewhere. He came to Kevin, and Kevin's response was:

"I think you should look at it very seriously. I think you should take them up on their invitation to fly you to Toronto, and here's the five questions you should ask them."

That team member took the job, and when he left, it was a celebration. Kevin was losing his right-hand man, and he couldn't have been happier because it was the best thing for his friend. Before leaving, this team member gave Kevin a list of ten incredibly able people whom he recommended to take his job, and one of those was hired. That person also left three years later to grow his career.

Instead of saying "we had two people leave, both only lasting three years each,' I looked at it as 'we had superstar performance for three years, then superstar performance for the next three years." And, guess who are our biggest advocates of Pharmasave? Those two people that left. So, if you truly subscribe to 'learn, grow, and win,' you can't let it choke you when you're going to lose someone. You've got to give them the freedom to leave. They'll go out and spread the word.

All of these events sent powerful messages across the company. Everyone knew that Kevin had their best interests at heart, no matter what. They also knew that they were responsible for their results and for resolving their own problems. Kevin would support them and help if they needed it, but it was their responsibility and they were accountable. That level of support built commitment and loyalty that could not be bought at any price, and boosted personal power phenomenally. The results speak for themselves, and they come from Kevin's formula:

Strong individuals lead to strong team leads to strong program.

Retail – Margaret Armour

Margaret Armour started Aerobics First in 1989 to sell shoes to runners and other athletes. Since then, it has grown to include equipment and accessories for skiing, snowboarding and other boarding sports. Margaret discovered that most of her customers found her by word of mouth. In a core market of 300,000 people, she has a database of 30,000 preferred customers, or Friends of Aerobics First (FOAF). Aerobics First has always used innovative marketing – they do no advertising and they don't put anything on a special or sale price – but the real key to their success in marketing lies in how Margaret manages and leads her employees.

What Aerobics First sells is not really relevant. What sets it apart is *how* it sells, and the philosophy that lies behind its approach. This way of doing business has allowed Margaret to hold her own against much bigger competitors – and some of those competitors even refer hard-to-cater-to customers to Margaret because they can't meet their needs with their mass-market approach.

I consider one of our drivers the fact that we're a knowledge-based reseller. We're selling people a lot of information. People like choices for things that they do for fitness and for recreation based on our knowledge of the product. We're very active in the sports that we're selling product for. We know about these sports. We know how the product works.

Vision and Values

Margaret's reasons for being in business are very clear. They are constantly communicated and reinforced in her people. She's not there to make money by selling things to a customer. She's there to build a relationship with them and to serve them.

The relationship with the customer is in many ways a sacred trust that you can abuse. I never once had to worry about what I sold people because I felt like I was selling people more joy in their life. In my

125

business, I'm selling things that people can use to develop their fitness. That is so important in the world we live in, with people's levels of stress and people's levels of busyness. Their sanity is tied up sometimes with their fitness. Those moments are about the ultimate quality of people's existence. My business in selling them their clothing and their shoes helps that.

Same with skiing and snowboarding. They make people's lives more sane, more fun. We sell them the safety and the tools and the equipment and make this thing work best for them. People can buy stuff cheaper somewhere else. But if people commit more, they want to deal with people who know what they're selling and actually have a passion for the product. That's who we are. It's easy to sell when you're selling these kinds of things and you're selling for these kinds of reasons. Sometimes on a busy Saturday here, particularly in the fall when people are getting ready for Christmas and for the winter season, it's very, very jovial. This is a fun thing. Even though it's a shopping day, and people are doing their errands, people are buying and planning what is going to be the fun thing in their lives. So it's a very carnival-like atmosphere. They're excited and you can be excited with them and for them.

Translating Vision and Values Into Action

In order to infuse her entire operation with this perspective, Margaret seeks out people who love the sports that she supplies, and she finds ways to augment their salaries with their own desires, aligning their goals. They don't have to be good at the sports they do – they just have to love them. She has never paid on commission because commission would create absolutely the wrong environment for her store as a knowledge-based reseller.

Retail notoriously doesn't pay high wages. It actually allows people who love these sports to come in contact with the very latest of the equipment related to these sports. That's number one. Number two, what I always used to say to my staff is, "this may be a part-time job for you while you go to school, but like everything you do in life you should embrace it with a full passion. You're here putting in hours, earning a salary. Why not make it work for you on a number of levels? That would be engaged fully in the whole process. Engaged fully in finding out as much as you can about the product that you're selling.

126

Chapter 8 – Leading the Way

Engaged fully with the customers that come in, in terms of really trying to meet their needs and serve them." We have a wonderful customer base. I often said to the staff that "theoretically your next job could be coming from the customer base that you're waiting on in the store." That has proven to be true on more than one occasion.

I've had a tremendous number of wonderful staff work at Aerobics First. Not everybody stays. Everybody has contributed. I've had a few who have said "I want to make a career of this," and have actually grown up and worked in the business for quite a while and then moved on in this industry. It's like anything in life – there's something to be gotten out of it that can help you build your own next step in life. It's your attitude about what it is you're doing.

Over the years, Margaret has brought some unexpected people into her business. She has had two kinesiologists running her shoe department. Normally kinesiologists would have nothing to do with retail sales, but she found people who were able to learn from running their own department and they brought phenomenal expertise in for her customers. When it came time for them to move on, she coached and supported them in building the next steps in their careers.

Margaret creates an environment that asks her people to contribute in innovative ways, to share what they're learning, to comment on what they saw, to find ways to improve things, and to take initiative and responsibility for that. She builds her training around encouraging that thinking, and she recognizes and rewards it.

Breaking the Micro-Management Trap

Ironically, entrepreneurs are just as likely as managers in large organizations to micro-manage, though for different reasons. Entrepreneurs love what they do, and so they want to be involved in everything. Thus they can have a great deal of trouble letting go, which can greatly reduce the personal power of their employees.

It is a major, major problem. It really is. It's about letting go and not even checking in or checking back, really giving people the authority to act on the responsibilities that they're given. Managing others and parenting are the two things that people fall in to that all they have are their own experiences. You often parent how you were parented,

127

although people will say to you "I don't want to be a parent like I was parented." A lot of the entrepreneurs will say to me, "I started my own business because I never liked working for anyone. I never liked how I was treated." They wind up acting the same way to their people. It's just a habit. You fall back into it because, to break that pattern, you have to learn a whole new skill set, and often it takes a lot of deep work at the personal level about "what are your attitudes about power? What does it mean to really let go? What is it you have to give up to let go?"

As detailed in Michael Gerber's book, *The E-Myth*, when you start a business, there are many different hats you have to wear. What took you into the business was the love of doing something, but once you're in business, you also have to work *on* the business, not just *in* it.

It seems the biggest challenge in managing people is to find the time to give to your staff. A lot of entrepreneurs just want to drop someone into the job and hope it works. They're too busy doing, doing, doing, to actually take the time. I think that once you begin to build a business and it involves others than yourself, your biggest role is more the communicator. They're doing your role.

Your staff are your first customers. They are ultimately the people that are going to interface with your customers, so how you interface with them is going to help them grow to the point where they represent you in a way that you want to be represented with your customers. When I wasn't in my store on a Friday night, and I'd worked there all week, I had to believe that who was down there working was going to do even better than me in meeting the needs of my customers when I wasn't there. In order for that to happen, I had to encourage that.

Building the Systems

Margaret has created a culture of constant learning in her organization that engages her people. She trains them in what to do, and gives them the power to act.

It's a shared journey. You have to invite someone into the process and then you have to give them feedback. You might have someone work with you for a few weeks, and then you sit them down and you give very specific feedback about what you see, and what you're feeling. You give them an opportunity to act on that feedback and incorporate it into how they might do differently. If you don't tell people what it is you're looking for, they don't know what your expectations are, then they can't move in that direction. You can't bring someone along and give them the responsibility and then be this seagull-type manager that swoops in and dumps all over how they're doing it.

Margaret no longer manages the store day-to-day. That has been passed on to someone who started working with her part-time 13 years ago.

Part of my role in the last while has been to bring along the next level of management. The biggest learning for me is that whole piece of letting go. He's grown up under my tutelage, but he is who he is and he has a way of doing things that is different from me. I can say that, in some things, he is far better than I ever was. Do I see things that he does that I just go, "oh, I'd do that differently?" Yes, I see that all the time. But it's not about me putting myself in there and saying "I think you should do it this way," or "do it this way." I support him and challenge him, but I can't undermine him, or take back that responsibility or the authority that I'm investing in him. I'm trying to create, with him, especially, the responsibility for delivering the results. Can he manage the inventory? Can he satisfy the customer?

This philosophy of letting go extends to all of her staff. A customer came in once with blisters from a ski boot he had bought the previous season. The clerk checked and found that he had been fitted for the wrong boots the year before. He exchanged the old boots for the correct pair. Then he gave the customer back the change, because the correct boots were cheaper than the wrong ones – which he had used for a year. That staff member was celebrated and recognized, because he did exactly what Margaret would have done.

Thanks to her customer database, Margaret knows exactly what that customer – and every other one of her 30,000 preferred customers – has invested in her store over the years. Given the lifetime value of that customer, and the goodwill this act produced, it was the best marketing investment Aerobics First could have made. Compare and contrast that treatment with the host of other retail operations that have massive policy manuals, or that search the belongings of staff to ensure they're not stealing anything when they leave. The cost of not respecting and not supporting the staff is staggering.

Letting go and supporting your people does involve a significant amount of change, whether you are an entrepreneur or a manager in any organization. It calls for a dedicated investment of time and effort and self-exploration. The payback is phenomenal for all involved.

I had a friend, a personal friend in her 50's who has achieved highly in other areas of her life to the point of having a doctorate and was a tenured university professor. She has moved out into the entrepreneurial world and has started a business, and she has told me without a doubt it is the single hardest thing she has ever done in her life. Just the challenge of it is unbelievable. She was getting her doctorate while she was working full-time and raising a family, so she was pretty stressed at that time in her life, but she said it was nothing compared to trying to make a small business work.

In many ways the entrepreneur journey is a journey of powerful, personal transformation. I welcome it in my life, and I like to support others that are stepping onto that path.

Public Sector – Ed Arsenault

I first met Ed Arsenault when he was a Lt. Colonel in the Canadian Air Force. As the Wing Logistics Officer for CFB Greenwood, he looked after all the support services for the base, from transportation and plumbers to communications and engineering services. Like much of the military, they had been heavily hit by cutbacks, losing as much as half of their people and budgets. Now the support side of the base had to bid against private sector firms to keep their jobs. Under Ed's direction, they reinvented their way of doing business to be competitive with private sector bids. To do so, he broke most of the 'rules' in the book, even those for this type of radical redesign.

Shortly after this, Ed left the military to work for a private sector transportation company, and he is now in charge of procurement for a school board. In both positions he has brought his laid back, open style to cutting through red tape and politics and finding the simple, elegant solutions that work.

Chapter 8 – Leading the Way

How to Work Hand-in-Hand With the Union

Like many organizations in the 1990's, the military faced huge cuts, and then were challenged to do things cheaper and faster with fewer people. Ed also faced something called Alternate Service Delivery, or ASD, which called for what was left of his side of the base to compete for their jobs against private sector bids.

We brought in consultants, looked at, at ways of doing things a lot smarter. We spent a lot of time overcoming the management-union interface problems that we'd had over several years. We really got down to a point where there was little money so we had to get along with the union and they had to get along with us or the potential was there to lose many more jobs to Alternate Service Delivery.

In an environment where the workforce had been totally demoralized by all the cuts, Ed put the chance to keep the remaining jobs into the hands of his people. He gave them back power that had been dashed by the cuts.

At the beginning, the union was really suspicious that Ed was out to cut more jobs. To show his honest intention and commitment, Ed made a full-time commitment to co-chair the steering committee with the president of the union. This committee was made up of equal numbers of management (military) and union representatives. In fact, Ed made sure the most vocal members of the union were on the steering committee. All of these actions were in total defiance to the directives of the existing chain of command. Ed took these actions because he knew they were the right things to do.

This joint structure meant that we would have no secret meetings with management or with union, we would open up all of our books, and show them what things really did cost. When we got a directive from Air Command to either cut positions or cut money or whatever, we would work around the table, and meet everyday, full time until we got it sorted out. This approach brought the union into the problem and into the process of finding solutions.

In the 1990's, re-engineering came to be known as a way to downsize. *Real* re-engineering is about reinventing the way you do work to enhance productivity, and if you free up additional resources (including people) you re-allocate them into other value-adding functions. Ed and his team did *real* re-engineering by guaranteeing that everyone at the end of the day would have a job in the plan they developed if they won the bid. The job just may not be the one they had now. That guarantee allowed the union to come on board.

In order to do the detailed redesign, the steering committee set up a number of smaller teams to address each problem, allowing more of the people affected to have a hand in designing their future.

We didn't appoint a specific leader for each of the design teams. We just let natural leadership emerge. What we discovered, for example, was that we might have a carpenter on the base, who, in his spare time, was vice president of refereeing for volleyball, or was a local Fire Chief in a volunteer fire department, where he had the opportunity to hone his leadership skills. In a lot of design teams, those natural leaders just emerged and in most cases, they weren't the people that you would have picked at the start of the process. Based on their unique perspectives, their solutions were phenomenal, I mean they would come up with some really creative and workable solutions. They clearly wanted the process to work for both sides.

Even in an environment where fear and oppression were dominant, by aligning goals with the union and the employees, and making the gap relevant to all concerned, he built the commitment and passion of the entire support side of the base. They completed their redesign on schedule and within the constraints set out by the air force.

The Power of Flexible Planning

In planning, Ed usually works with a five-year time frame to guide himself, and he makes sure he leaves enough flexibility to change his route along the way, because things can change very quickly. Ed finds it critically important to stay focused on where he's going, and to let the past go.

The first thing that I try <u>not</u> to do is drive looking in the rearview mirror. You can't do anything about things that are behind you, you can't do anything about. It doesn't do a lot of good to keep rehashing that stuff. I just pick the good parts out of that and then just let it to rest. The real fun is in front of you!

132

Chapter 8 – Leading the Way

While Ed finds it useful to research and plan to some extent, he doesn't plan every detail of the way. He identifies his key milestones, gets the basic information he needs to get started and then gets going. Ed learned this during a posting with NATO.

Aside from living in Europe for two years the job there as part of a NATO Planning Staff was tedious because all we did was plan. We would look at every scenario that we thought could possibly happen and then come up with plans for each one of those scenarios. Well that was futile because you knew if there was ever a crisis, it would likely be exactly what you didn't plan. There is a very wise expression that if the path in front of you looks familiar, it's probably not your path! What you have to do is make sure that you have the skills to do a lot of last minute planning and be flexible and adjust and make sure that the people that you work with have those same skills. That's what really builds a winning team. It's not having all of the plans in a cabinet that you can draw out and use when you have to. Above all, we must stay creative and flexible, and listen to everyone on the team.

To me we should have spent our time teaching people ways to solve things creatively, teaching brainstorming, how to be creative, as opposed to trying to figure out every possible situation. Because every crisis that happens has never been predictable. They have always been something that was completely out of the blue. That's why they were crises.

Bureaucracy kills creativity and flexibility. Those structures are designed to reduce or eliminate variance and eliminate risk. Bureaucracy is about controlling actions, as opposed to setting up the system and allowing your people to take the action required. It takes away personal power and it decreases productivity. What's more, it's simply impossible to write policy fast enough to cover every contingency. It's a hopeless, self-sabotaging effort.

Ed sets firm deadlines into his plans. While the path may be flexible, the deadline is not.

We set the end date of when we wanted to have everything done and then we wouldn't let anything distract us from that. People said, "we need more time to study this," and we would say "how can you study that in a shorter time frame?" And they said, "we could have three study groups instead of one," and we said "do that." We didn't let anything drive us off that deadline.

Quite often higher levels in the organization would want more time to study your proposals. We'd say, "you study it, we're going to keep moving on." So quite often when they came back with observations, we'd already gone three steps beyond that. You can't lose focus on the time line.

Always keep your eye on the horizon. Always have a goal in mind and attack that goal in small steps. Don't wait until all the planning is done or you'll never get it done.

How to Cut Out Planning and Halve the Cost

At one point, an additional squadron was moved to Greenwood and a new hangar had to be built. Traditionally the engineering studies would have taken two or three years. Then every design change would have had to go back to National Defence Headquarters and then to the architect and then to the base and then to the users and so on and so forth. Each design change would probably have taken a month or two. Such processes kill personal power.

Ed used a process that was completely new to government called 'fast track design build.' The designers and the users (the people from the squadron who would use the building) explained what they wanted in a short document. Once the architect and the company to build it were chosen, they then designed the footings and did a rough sketch of the building. At that stage, instead of designing the entire building and all the heating systems and electrical systems and so on, they allowed that company to go ahead and put the footings in because they knew the basic footprint of the building they wanted. The rest was designed as it was built.

Instead of having all the changes take months going through National Defence Headquarters, the key people involved agreed to get back to each other within 24 hours using telephone, e-mails, and faxes. They also agreed to solve problems at the job site and not go to their lawyers every second day.

Chapter 8 – Leading the Way

That required a lot of trust. Our usual turnaround time for design changes was generally less than twenty-four hours. That was unheard of. The end result was that we put up that hangar in fourteen months at fifty percent of the usual cost. That task would traditionally have taken five years or more.

Ed passed this project on to a Lieutenant to manage on a daily basis, which then freed other people to do other jobs. Ed's job was to hold higher headquarters at bay until his people produced the results he knew they could. Once that happened, Ed's superiors were eager to find out how they had produced such outstanding results.

Like all managers, Ed had an umbrella of control, within which he could shield and support his people, growing their personal power until they could produce the results that he knew were possible. In his current job with the school board, he was asked to implement a complicated new software program. He put his foot down, and only implemented one part of it because he knew forcing the whole package on them would overload and stress them. By learning one part of the program at a time, his people are mastering the program while people in other areas were overloaded and ended up accomplishing little because they tried to do too much.

Every manager has an umbrella of control. It may be small, but it is there. And that is where you can support your people and build their personal power to build the results they are capable of achieving. The size of this area of control really has more to do with the size of your own personal risk muscle than anything else. If you're uncomfortable taking chances, or if you have a highly stressed and worn-out workforce, you need to start small. Like any muscle, it needs to be built up, and the surest way to fail is to take too big a step. Ed has a strong risk muscle and trusted himself to take bigger chances, and so he got bigger results. That takes time to develop.

Why Sharing Information is Key

Many managers feel uncomfortable sharing information. It's not something that managers are supposed to 'do' in the traditional model.

I suppose that knowledge is supposed to be power and if you have the knowledge of what things cost, and you don't share, that supposedly safeguards your position. I tell people what things cost because I would rather have the trust of my employees. With this trust comes creative, team-based problem solving.

Sharing of information goes both ways, and there are many benefits to asking for information or help as well.

I don't like going off and making decisions on my own without getting input from staff. The end result is that in about fifty percent of the cases, you end up making the wrong decision and wrong decisions cost money. Good advice, on the other hand, is free.

I've always worked with larger groups of people, and I found that making sure you ask people their opinion or advice, or just asking them how to do it, is what nurtures trust. Employees don't like management that are always telling them what to do without ever asking them for their opinion. I always found that mutual exchange of information builds trust. A lot of managers, for some reason, just haven't clued in to that yet. Maybe they are afraid of losing power or losing self esteem, or perhaps they think people will think less of them. But it's just the opposite! People think a lot more of you when you ask their opinion.

One thing to remember as a manager however, is that often, people will volunteer information, but they don't want to help make the decision. Well that's fine. That's why you get paid as a manager: to make those decisions.

Managers are responsible for ensuring that the results happen, not necessarily for making the results happen themselves. In the end, the results come not from focusing on the results themselves, but rather from supporting your people and enhancing their personal power.

When you look after people, everything else falls into place. Every business has to make a profit, but if you take care of the people, the profits will take care of themselves. I don't mean that to sound too flippant, but that's really what it takes. You treat people with respect, you keep them in the loop as to what's happening, you seek advice, you make good decisions, and the profit is something that flows out of the process.

Making It Work

Are these leaders perfect? Certainly not, and they would be the first ones to acknowledge it. What they all realize, however, is that results come from their people, not from the leader directly. They understand the paradox. The more you focus on the results alone, the poorer your results over time. The more you focus on enhancing the personal power of your people, the better your results. The buck does stop with the leader, and these leaders understand that the role of the leader is to build effective cultural systems that let their people deliver the results.

Leadership is a tricky thing. There is really no training for leadership other than effective mentoring and coaching while on the job. Despite this, people are placed in leadership positions and expected to be able to lead as if simply receiving the promotion endowed them with some intuitive, magical ability to lead. In most organizations, it is not acceptable to speak of the Emperor's new clothes and admit you don't know everything about how to lead, so people just do the best they can and try to muddle through. The higher up you go, the harder it can be to admit your doubt about your own abilities. It's little wonder that executives' greatest fear is being exposed as an imposter.

If you are to improve, you have to measure your own effectiveness. You have to know what you're doing well, and you have to know what *specific* actions you need to take to improve. You have to be able to quantify formerly abstract concepts such as leadership, personal power, and organizational culture, and that can be done. There are many effective leadership and organizational climate surveys that effectively concretize these abstract concepts. These measurements then point to your strategy for improvement. You need to keep measuring these numbers regularly and putting as much weight on them as you do the income statement and balance sheet.

Ironically, much of the discomfort people have with feedback on leadership is an artifact of the traditional, autocratic management that is so ineffective. In that model, feedback meant that you'd messed up and were in trouble, not that you had an opportunity to improve and grow.

There are three simple questions I would ask managers who are uncomfortable with looking at their own leadership abilities. First, are you perfect? Given that the answer to that is likely, 'no,' then, do you want to improve your leadership? If so, then how are you going to do that?

By this last question, I mean what *exactly* are you doing well and what *exactly* are your weaknesses, and how do you plan to improve those weaknesses – specifically? Which of your actions are increasing personal power and which are draining it for your people? How do you know?

In choosing to target your cultural systems and leadership, work with someone who has a proven track record for improving both leadership and organizational climate. Make sure that the people you work with can measure what they say and that they can coach you in developing your leadership ability.

Finally, be sure you are ready for addressing your culture and leadership. Redesigning the cultural systems in your organization, and building your leadership abilities and that of your managers is a major task that takes a real investment of time, money and resources. This course of action isn't a one-time event. It is a strategic change in direction and a way of doing business. You need to keep measuring these numbers on an ongoing basis, and holding yourself and your people as accountable for them as you do for financial figures. If you're uncertain of what to invest, apply the StressCosts Formula™. to your organization to find out what stress is costing you right now. What ROI would you need to make it an effective investment?

If you're not ready to address the root causes of stress, your cultural systems and leadership, then you can invest in programs that enhance the personal power of your people. Simply helping your individual employees can produce significant results. You have to decide what you are ready to do, and how much recovering the productivity lost to stress is worth to you. You now know what that costs you in dollars and cents. It's your call.

Index

85/15 rule, 69

A

absenteeism, 7, 8, 9, 11, 12, 17,
    19, 22, 23, 26, 36, 41, 43, 46,
    47, 52, 55, 59, 65, 66, 67, 70,
    91, 116
accountability, 88, 92
accountable, 83, 88, 92, 93, 95,
    97, 109, 124, 138
administrative, 21, 41
administrative support, 41
adrenal glands, 33
Aerobics First, 125, 129
    Friends of Aerobics First
        (FOAF), 125
Albany Times Union, 71
alcohol, 8, 35, 36, 37, 52
Alternate Service Delivery, 131
alternative work arrangements, 48
ambiguity, 55
American Institute of Stress, 19
amygdala, 32, 33
annual growth, 74
anxiety, 24, 26, 35, 52, 54
Aon Consulting, 60
Armour
    Margaret, 125
Arsenault
    Ed, 130
arteriosclerosis, 36
arthritis, 36
asthma, 36
Australia, 27
Australian Confederation of
    Trades Union, 27
autonomy, 55, 56
Aventis, 27
awards, 96

B

back problems, 36
bank, 82, 97, 99
baseline, 65, 73, 112
benefits, 11, 15, 21, 23, 24, 47, 56,
    60, 61, 65
blood pressure, 32, 36, 43
BLS Survey of Occupational
    Injuries and Illnesses, 41
blue-collar, 24
brain cells, 36
Brazil, 27
bullying, 8
Bureau of Labor Statistics, 26
bureaucracy, 83, 86, 98, 103, 104,
    133
burnout, 58
business planning, 116

C

C.E.O. Goals, 90, 95
CA, 71
caffeine, 37
call center, 23, 99, 100, 101
    inbound, 99
    outbound, 99
Canada, 18, 27, 37, 42, 43, 51, 54,
    60
Canada @ Work, 60
Canada Life, 66
cancer, 8, 36, 54
cardiovascular disease, 8, 17, 25,
    36, 52, 54
career mobility, 44
Career Systems International, 56
CBI. See Confederation of British
    Industry

145

W

About the Author

Ravi Tangri has designed and implemented effective innovation across North America. His success comes from building commitment throughout the organization and making the innovation relevant to the employees who have to make it work. Ravi is a founder of Chrysalis Performance Strategies Inc. He developed Chrysalis' Stress Elimination Technology™, which has reduced absenteeism by over 27%. He is the creator of Chrysalis' breakthrough facilitation process, *Genesis*, used to build the cultural systems that recover productivity lost to stress.

Chrysalis Performance Strategies Inc.

Chrysalis is a leader in creating effective innovation. With its unique *Genesis* facilitation process, Chrysalis helps to create innovation that is relevant to both your customers and to the employees who will make that innovation work.

Chrysalis grows productivity by building the personal power of your employees, directly through the *Thriving In Chaos* Program, and indirectly by coaching your leaders with *Relevance Coaching*.

You succeed by tapping your employees' passion and aligning it with your corporate and customer goals. Chrysalis helps you make that happen.

Thriving In Chaos

The program proven to increase personal power and decrease absenteeism by up to 27%

"The sick leave for our employees who completed the *Thriving In Chaos* program measured a 27% decrease, and equivalent increase in productivity which more than paid for the program in a period less than six months."

Jerry Dodson, SNSMR

Overall, *Thriving In Chaos* graduates:

- are much better able to manage themselves in stressful situations
- significantly reduce their physical and mental symptoms of ill-health
- are much better able to leave work at work and home at home
- have a stronger positive attitude
- have increased job satisfaction

"Our industry has been going through one massive change after another, almost on a daily basis at times. Our team is the best there is at this, and even then the pressure was affecting them. We were concerned about making budget, but with Chrysalis, we actually over-achieved plan."

**Catherine DeSua, General Manager,
Fraser & Hoyt Corporate Travel**

CHRYSALIS
PERFORMANCE STRATEGIES INC.

Create a Healthy, Productive Workplace by Rebuilding Your Cultural Systems and Leadership

Genesis

Genesis is Chrysalis' unique, breakthrough facilitation process, based on the creative strategy of Walt Disney himself. It allows you and your team to create the innovation you need, including:

- rebuilding your cultural systems to enhance personal power
- redesigning your strategy
- developing new products and services

By involving your entire organization at key points in the process, *Genesis* builds buy-in, commitment, accountability, and personal power as it creates the results that you need.

Relevance Coaching

Relevance Coaching helps you and your leaders build your supportive management practices and grow their employees' personal power. We can start by measuring leadership skills to identify what behaviours need to change and to set measurable targets for improvement. Then, using our F.A.S.T. Track System (Focus, Accountability, Systems and Targets), we help you build your skills and chart your progress.

For more information on *Thriving In Chaos*, *Genesis* and/*or* *Relevance Coaching*, contact Chrysalis at:

Toll-Free: 1.888.5.CHRYSALIS (1.888.524.7972)
Web: www.Stress-Cures.com
e-mail: Team@TeamCHRYSALIS.com

ISBN 141200074-2